SELF
IN
INTEGRAL EVOLUTIONARY MYSTICISM:

TWO MODELS
AND
WHY THEY MATTER

Self in Integral Evolutionary Mysticism:
Two Models and Why They Matter

Marc Gafni

Edited by Heather Fester

Integral Publishers
Tucson, Arizona

Integral Publishers
1418 N. Jefferson Ave.
Tucson, AZ 85712
(831) 333-9200

© 2014 Integral Publishers
First Printing: September 2014

ISBN: 978-0-9896827-8-7

Cover Design by Jeannie Carlisle

Published in the United States with printing and distribution in the United States, United Kingdom, Australia and the European Union.

TABLE OF CONTENTS

CHAPTER 1:

FRAMEWORKS MATTER

Charles Taylor in his classic work *Source of Self* reminded us that frameworks matter because frameworks are foundational, and the foundations affect just about everything else. Particularly critical, insists Taylor, is the model or framework for Self. In a post-traditional world, new frameworks of meaning are being established by those on the leading edge of thought. There is enormous privilege and responsibility in articulating and enacting new source code frameworks of meaning. Not only substance, but nuance, tone, and flavor matter. We need genuine dharma dialogue to clarify important distinctions in our core frameworks.

A deeper discussion of frameworks or what I might simply call context or prism through which reality is understood and enacted in daily life seems therefore worthwhile before we engage our essential inquiry, the distinction between two models of self and why they matter.

It is at this particular moment in history that frameworks matter more then ever. We live in a web of ubiquitous lies. As cultural critic Brad Blanton and many others have pointed out, in many significant ways marketing has replaced meaning and commodification has replaced genuine communion and commitment. Or to say it more starkly, lying is a way of life, and the sense of any form of ultimate truth is greatly eroded. This is true in economics, politics, religion, and even in the once more pure world of alternative spirituality. The commodification of spirit has spread from organized religion to the world of Internet marketing that drives so much of the new spiritual, fitness, and health and wellness worlds. Despite, or sometimes even because of, all the grand claims, it is difficult to get hold of a genuine truth sense. There is a pervasive sense that there is little that has ultimate value, and particularly a genuine post-postmodern sense of self, purpose, and obligation remains elusive at best. At the same time, virtually every social critic correctly recognizes that it is precisely these maps of meaning that align our life purpose not only with success, but also with significance. More than that, repeated studies show that the average Westerner believes in some form of God, higher spirit, or meaning. But what that is remains at the best elusive and more often than not, confusing. it is therefore, not genuinely instructive or inspiring for enacting a life that cogently serves the good, the true, and the beautiful.

When Taylor reminded us that we all live in inescapable frameworks, he was articulating the best of post-postmodern realization. It was not a cry of despair, but a wake-up call which demands that we take seriously the passionate—and what we might even term, the ecstatically urgent—need to explicate and clearly articulate our implicit frameworks of meaning and particularly of self. The articulation of a compelling vision of post-dogmatic meaning is the key goal of each institute within our think tank, the Center for Integral Wisdom. Each institute addresses a specific pivotal domain in our public or private lives. One of our most important domains is that of a post-dogmatic universal spirituality which transcends and includes the core wisdom of each of the great traditions. This is the mission of the World Spirituality Project within the Center for Integral Wisdom, whose purpose is to articulate a World Spirituality based on Integral principles, that transcends and includes the best of pre-modern, modern, and postmodern realization.[1]

MORE ON FRAMEWORKS

Reality is virtually never confronted directly; rather, it is engaged through a prism or a framework. Another way to say it is a framework is a perspective through which we engage reality. In the pre-modern and modern period, when we human beings used to think we were engaging reality as it is, each religion felt that its insights were absolute truth. At the same time, they held that the perceptive faculties of other religions were somehow distorted or inferior to their own. The great realization of postmodernity, emergent from the epistemology of Kant, is that ordinary consciousness cannot engage reality without the prism of perspective. Every individual and every human being has a perspective. To put it another way, reality itself is fundamentally constructed from perspectives. Perspectives are irreducible, and at the same time, always mediated through larger contexts. All of reality is contexts within contexts. Context is, simply put, the constant matrix for perspective. The pre-modern mistake was the failure to realize that every religion emerged in a very specific context, which had a very particular perspective. Therefore, no religion had a right to claim that its intuition of truth was either ultimate or exclusive, and yet, that's precisely what every religion did.

That is where a lot of the trouble that undermined the credibility of spirit in the modern and postmodern world began. When the truths of all the great traditions were gathered, they were in many respects contradictory. Each claimed to know directly an exclusive set of truth claims that were contradicted by the other religions. A simple example among dozens would be the dogmatic Christian claim that eternal salvation was *only* available through the

---

1 See the articles by M. Gafni, "Essential World Spirituality Teaching" (2011) and "Ten Commitments of a World Spirituality Based on Integral Principles" (2013), both available at www.ievolve.org.

acceptance of Jesus as the Christ. This caused much of modernity and most of postmodernity to reject the great traditions. After all, every tradition was claiming absolute truth, and the claims contradicted one another. Initially this was a major contributing factor in the rejection of the great traditions. A second factor was the failure of the religions themselves to distinguish between their own surface structures and depth structures. By surface structure, I refer to rituals and dogma which were asserted as true, but not empirically experienced as true through the enactment of practice, and therefore, not subject to third-person verification. The context of a religion was sometimes a pivotal variable informing the surface structures of the religion. Historical, cultural, topographical, economic, and other factors often had significant influence on the surface structures of rituals, rites of passage, holy days, and beliefs. Context also influenced some dimension of the depth structure. For example, a Hindu, a Jew, and a Christian doing the same practice for accessing the divine feminine might each access her presence in a different garb, with the Hindu seeing Parvati, Lakshmi, or Kali; the Jew seeing the Shechina in the image of a widow weeping at the wailing wall in Jerusalem; and the Christian seeing Mother Mary. Depth structures refer to precisely those assertions that were arrived at through practices to open the eye of the spirit, and therefore, were subject to third-person verification by others engaging in the same practices. Nonetheless, the eye always sees through a prism. The prism affects both how the depth structures manifest in the world as well as some of the texture of the depth structure itself. We now understand that the medium and the message are inextricably intertwined. Even with this established insight, there is still a significant dimension of depth structures that transcend context conditioning and are a reflection of the universal essences shared by all the great traditions.

The Unique Self of a Religion

A great deal of the depth structures are shared between the great traditions, but not all of them. A depth structure is also the production of the irreducibly unique perspective of that religion which, while mediated by context, is not in any way reducible to merely context. The distinction between surface structures and depth structures, coupled with the postmodern realization that every great tradition and culture perceived essence through a particular perspective, allows us to avoid the tragic mistake of deconstructing the traditions as meaningless. Deconstruction wrongly assumed that when perspective is revealed to be part of the process of meaning-making, there is no longer any real meaning. Perspectives may be taken to indicate a plentitude rather than a paucity of meaning. From this point, we can understand the perspective of every great religion as true but partial. This understanding need not lead to a leveling of differences between traditions. All perspectives are true but partial, and it may also be fairly said that each authentic perspective incorporates, or more accurately discerns and reflects, a unique dimension of the true, good, or beautiful view of reality.

The unique perspective of every religion is what I might term the Unique Self of the religion.[2] This Unique Self of a religion—mediated through its core contexts—helped form a cultural worldview. This worldview was the framework through which reality was lived, through which our ethical calculus evolved, and through which meaning was made. Each worldview told a story, a grand narrative. How each narrative understood the role of the personal or the individual, was of enormous consequence. It was a key pivoting point, which affected everything else in the narrative. The status of the individual was virtually always a central factor in establishing values, ethics, and obligations.

---

2   We will naturally discuss some dimensions of Unique Self in this book. However, for a more complete understanding of Unique Self, see *Your Unique Self* (2012, Integral Publishers); *JITP* 6.1, the *Awakening Your Unique Self* telecourse (2013); and the *Wake Up, Grow Up, Show Up, and Participate in the Evolution of Love* telecourse (2013). Both telecourses can be accessed on www.ievolve.org and at http://uniqueself.com/unique-self-courses/. A complete timeline of the Unique Self teaching evolution is also available in Appendix C of this book and on the Unique Self website at http://uniqueself.com/unique-self-timeline/.

For a significant sector of humanity, religions no longer play that role. Religion is no longer the explicit, nor for many, the implicit framework for meaning making. Worldviews are often not explicit, and even when implicit, not rooted in religions, or at least not rooted solely in religion. Grand narratives, to the extent that they exist at all for the leading edge of democratic pluralistic people, are often not sourced in spirit. Moreover, for most of postmodernity, the only grand narrative was that there was no grand narrative. The one universal of postmodernity was the paradoxically dogmatic assertion that there were no universals. Of course, this is an implicitly contradictory claim that has been referred to as a performative contradiction. That simply means that the claim that there are no universals is itself a dogmatic universal claim.[3] T h i s realization and others have led us into post-postmodernity. As we move into post-postmodernity, a new movement is arising which, after internalizing the wisdom of deconstruction, is initiating a new reconstructive project. This movement seeks to integrate partial truths of all the great systems gnosis into a new and more complete integral framework. The thinkers within this movement have the courage to stand in the breach and articulate a new story of patterns that connect. It is the simple truth that the classical sources of cultural wisdom, the academy and churches, are not addressing the core challenge to meaning. Now, new visions of the patterns that connect are emerging. The old churches are either pre-modern or fig leafs for an insipid relativism, failing to articulate a vision that either compels or inspires. The academy is paralyzed in two core ways. First, it is for the most part under the sway of various forms of scientism, which see narrow sensory empiricism and rational-deductive method as the only true source of gnosis. Second, departments virtually all focus on their narrow area of specialization so that links between arenas of knowledge, meta-theories, or grand narratives are met with dogmatic disdain and dismissal. So, it remains for Integral visionaries on the leading edge to engage in the age-old practice that once belonged to the

3 Important writers in this vein include Thomas Nagel, Charles Taylor, Jurgen Haabermaas Huston Smith, and Ken Wilber.

great traditions, the articulation of meta-frameworks and the formulation of meta-theory. A particularly powerful expression of this impulse is the initiation of a World Spirituality based on Integral Principles which, as previously stated, transcends and includes the best of pre-modern, modern, and postmodern thought into a larger post-postmodern Integral framework. In World Spirituality, a new vision of freedom and obligation are emergent as the awakening of the evolutionary Unique Self within an evolutionary we space.

In the pre-modern world, there were religious wars for three core reasons. First, there were the most base of human motivations: greed, egoic power, and grasping. Second, each religion thought they were absolutely right and were thus fighting for the sake of God and truth. They were unaware that they were seeing reality through a prism and had little sense of the distinctions between surface structures and depth structures. Third, and this is the most often forgotten point in liberal circles, people fought because ideas, one's view of the interior nature of reality, was understood to matter, and to matter ultimately.

Today, we are standing in the place of the great traditions. We must articulate new frameworks of meaning. We now understand that so much ostensibly religious contestation over ideas was regressive and primitive, rooted either in egoic power agendas or inappropriate pre-modern claims to exclusive truth. However, we must reclaim the responsibility for contestation for a very different reason. One's interior view of reality does ultimately matter. That view of the interior face of the cosmos is the implicit framework in which life, love, and meaning are enacted. Frameworks matter. Frameworks are at their core the interior perspectives through which we see reality. So frameworks are foundational, as stated above. A weakness in the foundation has dramatic effects on the entire edifice. Frameworks matter ultimately. Frameworks are not only mediated by ephemeral and relative contexts, they also create essential contexts in which we live and love, including but not limited to our moral context. Frameworks create the meta-meanings that shape the very fabric of our lives and commitments.

This is particularly and poignantly true if we are indeed on the leading edge of the post-postmodern world, catalyzing the emergence of new meta-frameworks. If, as so many of us in the Integral communities often claim somewhat grandly, we are indeed creating the future, as expressions of the evolutionary impulse, then we are creating the moral contexts for the future. This is a great and awesome responsibility, which requires gravitas and courage. To borrow the Sanskrit word, *dharma* matters. We have to take our dharma responsibility seriously. We need genuine dharma debate and dialogue to clarify important distinctions. It is all about deploying the best faculties of perception, available through the eye of the spirit and the eye of the heart, to articulate a new framework of meaning.

It is for this reason that in this essay I feel called, even obligated, to engage, if only in broad brush strokes, a foundational issue in the source code of Integral thinking, the nature of the self. A pivotal issue of momentous significance in creating a moral context is the relationship between autonomy and communion, self and other. The quality and texture of intersubjective engagement in virtually every major developmental model is the litmus test of evolving consciousness. This, in turn, depends heavily on one's model of self.[4]

The dialogue between the two models of self that we discuss in this book must be held in the spirit of honor and love, with academic rigor and open heart, much like the Talmudic scholars in the study hall engaged in *havruta*. These scholars, who look like they are "battling fiercely and thrusting lances, leave the study hall as beloveds."[5] These Talmudic battles were not egoic battles. They were not about turf or branding, but about a truly enlightened and egoless search for the most integral truth that could be realized. The multicultural and ostensibly pluralistic consciousness that fails to discern or create any value distinctions between alternative frameworks creates a new age potpourri of truths in which there is

---

4 This article is but a first step of an Integral theory of Self. A more complete discussion of an Integral theory of Self I hope to share in a forthcoming book co-authored with a leading Integral theorist.

5 *Tractate Kiddushin.*

no hierarchy, no genuine responsibility, no true sense of obligation, and of course, no compelling moral context. If the Integral framework is going to avoid being degraded into but another commodity in the marketplace hawking spirit, it must engage in genuine post-egoic loving dharma combat. In that spirit, this is a first foray into the burning question, what are the contours and textures of the emergent Integral Self? I will not cover this topic exhaustively, but will rather focus in this essay on one particular dimension of this issue. In a future essay, I hope to speak about this issue in a more complete manner.

Unique Self and Authentic Self in Context

Within the Integral context, two ways of thinking about self have emerged which are distinctive both in their shared contours and significant distinctions. One framework or model has been called Authentic Self, and the other, Unique Self.[6]

Clarification of the Term Unique Self

What I have termed Unique Self[7] shows up in all four quadrants of reality. These include the interior and exterior worldspaces of both the individual (I) and the collective (We). Unique Self is the deepest and most evolved interior experience of evolving selfhood. This is the interior worldspace of the individual. Unique Self shows up in the particularity of the exterior form of the individual, for example, in the unique cellular and atomic signature of every human being. This is the exterior worldspace of the individual. In the collective space, Unique Self shows up as legal construct within a legal system, as the self evident and inalienable rights of

---

6 The following emerged from a series of conversations between Ken Wilber and myself, which sought to clarify the term Unique Self. Some of these issues are more fully explicated in the scholarly treatment of Unique Self and in the footnotes there. See Gafni (2012, *YUS*) fn. 3, 13, 17, 21, 26, and 27. For nuanced discussion of these issues, see also Gafni (2012, *YUS*), footnote 1, Ch. 1.

7 To view the timeline of the term Unique Self in the history of my teaching, please view Appendix C. An updated version of this timeline is also maintained on the companion website to the *Your Unique Self* (2012) book: http://uniqueself. com/unique-self-timeline/.

the individual. This is in the exterior worldspace of the collective. Unique Self shows up as the currency of connection between individuals forming the connective tissue of interior we space. This is in the interior worldspace of the collective. Unique Self is also a primary form of typology. For example, the distinctly calibrated integration of the masculine and feminine types within every individual are a core expression of Unique Self. Said simply, no two hermaphrodites are the same.

Primarily, however, Unique Self appears as a distinct structure, level or stage (using these terms synonomously) and state or what Ken Wilber has called a state-stage of consciousness. By structure stage of consciousness I mean a distinct structure or level of consciousness that expresses particular levels in different lines of development. What is the difference between a level and a line? By line of development I mean, for example, conceptual thinking, values, moral, psycho-sexual and emotional development, as well as a series of other distinct lines of development. By level I refer to those distinct structure stages of consciousness that developmental theory in all of its forms has done a really good job of mapping in the last few decades. These are distinct and recognizable structure stages of consciousness. To cite but one example, in moral development a person moves through several levels of development. Three of the levels unfold as follows. The individual begins with egocentric love, care, and concern; evolves to ethnocentric love, care, and concern; and then evolves again to worldcentric love, care, and concern. At level one, his felt sense of love, care, and concern is only for himself and his immediate support system. At level two, his felt sense of love, care, and concern, expands to include his entire tribe, society, company, or nation. At level three, his felt sense of love, care, and concern expands again to include all human beings. The distinct structure stage at which Unique Self shows up for the first time as a spontaneous expression of self-consciousness is at the worldcentric level. This approximates what is known in spiral dynamics developmental theory as Graves level six, the rational, or in the color-coded schema, the orange world space. At an even higher or deeper level of consciousness, which is sometimes termed kosmocentric, one's identity shifts to an identity with all-that-is, and love, care, and concern expand to include all sentient beings. At this level, Unique Self is stabilized and deepened, showing up in even bolder and brighter relief.

Let me shift to second person to make the Unique Self realization at the level of kosmocentric consciousness even more clear. At this level of consciousness, you realize that you are an irreducibly unique expression of the love intelligence and love beauty that is the initiating and animating Eros of all-that-is, which lives in you, as you, and through you. The Universe is having a You experience. You are not separate from the Universe at all, even as you are a distinct expression of all-that-is. For example, if your name were Adam, you would experience the Universe as "Adaming."

Unique Self is thus primarily understood as a structure-stage of consciousness that one awakens to at a particular level of development. Unique Self, however, is also a highly realized state of consciousness—for example, during an ecstatic flow state—at earlier or later developmental stage. By state I refer to a transient expansion of one's consciousness (which when stabilized becomes a state-stage). For example one might talk about a mystical, drunken, or ecstatic state. The ultimate realization of an expanded state of consciousness is a shift in the understanding of one's true nature or essential identity, particularly the classical realization that one is not merely a separate self, but a True Self. True Self is the singular that has no plural, the total number of True Selves being one. Unique Self in its fullest expression is the unique perspective of True Self, and it is, therefore, a fully self-realized state of consciousness.

As I have pointed out over the years, at the level of Unique Self, the Integral theory distinction between states and structure-stages of consciousness melts into the larger One. The highest structure stage of self-consciousness is the fully realized Unique Self, which as we have said, begins to show up spontaneously at the worldcentric stage and is most fully awake, aware, and alive at the Kosmocentric stage. The highest state of consciousness is Unique Self as well, which is nothing other then the irreducibly unique perspective of

True Self. Unique Self is thus properly understood as the highest state of waking up and the highest stage of growing up.

Before proceeding, one other note is in order. In my work, I also deploy the term Unique Self in an entirely different way and assert that all form is unique, and therefore, there is Unique Self all the way up and all the way down the ladder of consciousness and complexity. It is simply true that every form has its own intrinsic uniqueness. So, in this sense, in early dialogues, both Ken and I have said things like all forms have a Unique Self. This deployment of the term Unique Self in these usages refers not to the Self-realized state or structure stage of consciousness, but rather to the essential uniqueness that form always exhibits once it emerges from emptiness. This might be termed unconsciousness or sleeping uniqueness. To avoid the confusion of double-dipping terms, Unique Self as it is classically deployed in my writing and in this essay in particular, virtually always refers to the structure-stage of Unique Self realization, which occurs most fully when Unique Self awakens as the unique perspective of True Self. This is the expression of Unique Self as both state and structure-stage of consciousness. This is awakened or conscious Uniqueness. This level of Unique Self appears not only deductively, but also as a spontaneous expression of self and self-identity. It would probably be clearer not to refer to other expressions of uniqueness as Unique Self because unique essence as the structure-stage of a developed and awakened self-quality does not come online until much higher stages of human development, both in terms of states and structure-stages.

By Way of Introduction:
A Crisis of Self, ReSelfing, or "Live Your Story" vs. "Move beyond Your Story"

Unique Self is about the active embrace and incarnation of your Self and Story. We have lost our mooring in Self and Story. In truth, we never fully had them. Unique Self is an evolutionary emergent. When I speak of Self, I do not refer to the contracted story of your ego self, which I often refer to as separate self. Your separate self experiences your story as separate from all-that-is, from nature, from source, from other and from your own depths. Rather, I refer to your Unique Self story as the unique expression of essence that arises as your sacred autobiography. Your Unique Self is the fully expanded and embraced story of all-that-is living in you, as you, and through you. You are not separate from all-that-is. That is the first-person experience of your Unique Self. It might be fairly said that the critical challenge of our age is a loss of sense of Self and Self Story. Self arises out of the non-dual realization of the seamless coat of the universe, not as the desiccated sculptures of Giacometti who are but skin encapsulated egos. We have lost the thread of our narrative and are unable to locate the infinite depth and dignity of our Unique Self story.

There are six major spiritual and cultural movements today that stand against the integrity of Self and Story. Each of their critiques of story are true but partial. All of their critiques of Self and Story are fully overcome in the theory and realization of Unique Self. By way of introducing this essay, I will list these six critiques. In a different article each of these critiques needs to be located in relation to the model of self it critiques, and within the larger framework of Integral distinctions.[8]

The first movement against Self and Story is sourced in Theravada Buddhism, but shows up in virtually all forms of classical enlightenment teaching of the variety taught at many spiritual centers around the world, which emphasizes the realization of what is often termed No-Self or True Self. This teaching moves a person past personality or ego and into the space of the unifying awareness or consciousness in which we all participate. This important teaching is true but partial. This teaching rejects story. The first thing you are told is to "give up your

---

8 In a dialogue with Sean Esbjörn-Hargens in the Unique Self Thought Leader Dialogue series, I identified these six movements against Self and Story, and Sean and I began mapping each of them within the Integral distinctions. See the Center for Integral Wisdom website at ievolve.org, and search Sean Esbjörn-Hargens and Marc Gafni, "Towards an Integral Theory of Self."

story" and "detach from desire." The teaching fails to distinguish between the pettiness of your ego's pseudo-story and the dignity of your authentic Unique Self story. The self that is rejected in this theory is the notion that there is any sense of essence in human separateness or uniqueness. These two qualities are virtually always conflated and seen as an illusion of conditioning, which is overcome through awakening to one's true nature, classically called enlightenment. Much more will be said in this regard below so these few sentences will suffice at this point.

The second movement against Self and Story is rooted in what has been called, in one version of developmental theory, Spiral Dynamics green level or Graves level six consciousness. (Clare Graves is the original architect of this developmental model. Each of the levels is identified with a particular color.[9]) This level is an extreme version of pluralism and multiculturalism. Of course, both are good and noble principles that express a genuine evolution in consciousness. They are based on the claim that distinctions are rooted in egoic contraction, and if we would move beyond ego and take the perspective of other, we would see their position as equally valid. No perspective, including your own, can actually have a priority or ontology. There is a rejection of all hierarchy, motivated by an obsession to level all differences. All differences are implicitly thought to derive from mistaken identity with your perspective. There is no sense that perspective might derive from Unique Self. So along with green level's appropriate rejection of hidden dominator hierarchies, which is characteristic of green consciousness, there is a loss of all discernment and authority rooted in authentic Unique Self authorship. The self that is rejected at this level is the individuated self who holds his own authority and who is qualitatively distinct in capacity and consciousness from other.

The third movement against story is a particular strain of Christian forgiveness and love. Forgiveness and love in this classical strain of church father teachings, is based on pure divine grace. The human self is not thought to be invested with

---

9   Graves, C. (1974). "Human nature prepares for a momentous leap." *The Futurist*. April.

sufficient adequacy to warrant the dignity of responsibility and therefore accountability. When such love and instant forgiveness is deployed cheaply, it undermines the value of moral hierarchy and the dignity of Self and Story. For example, when there is a massacre of schoolchildren, and there is instant forgiveness and love for the murderers, the basic structure of Self and Story as the lodestones of human adequacy are undermined.

The fourth movement against Self and Story is the academic dogma of postmodernism, which demands the deconstruction of all Self and Story lines. Story lines are said to be purely subjective signifiers which are context bound, socially constructed, and without any fragrance of Essence. Stories and Selves in this view are held to be without objective correlates with which they may be checked and validated. All is deconstructed. Self and Story are hopelessly undermined.

This fourth position is an extreme and absurd distortion of a correct and critical core insight—the realization that perspective and context have a significant impact on the self stories we tell about our lives and the world. The grand narrative claim of postmodernity is that there are no grand narratives. All narratives are deconstructed. The only story that remains, however, is that there is no story, and in this contradiction, extreme postmodernity is undermined.

The fifth movement against Self and Story is plain old flatland relativism, described by Lewis Mumford as the "disqualification of the Universe." This is the simple denial of any depth to reality. There is no moral depth. There is no qualitative depth. The world is a place of interacting post-systems theories. But, in this view, there can be no interiors which are valid realities deserving our attention. All acts are equally valid. All moral distinctions are held to be the construction of the human ego. There is no authentic ethical texture that can guide us, no genuine moral distinctions that can be authentically made about the nature of our lives or the quality of our actions.

The sixth and final movement against story and self is evolutionary spirituality. For evolutionary spirituality, the only true reality is the process. There is no true individual independent of the process. This critique that conflates dialectical materialism (evolutionary theory) and Advaita Vedanta (enlightenment teaching) is particularly popular in some Integral circles. In this theory, the only self that exists is authentic or sometimes referred to as evolutionary self, which is in effect a non-self, that is to say, which is essentially impersonal or without any essential personal quality. Although the term self is deployed, it is really an evolutionary version of no-self expressed as the ultimate primacy of the process. Only the process is real. I will unpack this critique of Self in some depth in this essay.

Each of these six movements levels an important and powerful critique of some version of the separate self or ego's story. Each, however, fails to distinguish the separate self story from the Unique Self story. Each creates significant potential destruction in its wake. When Self and Story are effaced, then human dignity is undermined and all manner of brutality becomes possible.

Beyond the denial of Self and Story is the distortion of Self and Story. The distortion of Self and Story, like its denial, is also a primary source of evil. The accurate rendition of narrative is holding multiple perspectives on Self and Story and being able to take a perspective on your own perspective as a primary source of goodness and love. The central characteristic of evil is not what the old books used to call sin. There is no righteous person in the land who does not sin. The character trait that creates evil is the refusal to tell the truth about the story. Evil claims a story without sin. The result is that the evil person almost always projects their darkness outward. This virtually always results in the demonization of other. The surest sign of individual evil or communal corruption is demonization and scapegoating. Since the demonizers refuse to take ownership of their own darkness, they must always perceive others as bad. Sister Terese of Lisieux wrote, "If you are willing to bear serenely the trial of being displeasing to your self, then you will for Jesus be a pleasant place of shelter."[10]

---

10 *Collected Letters of St. Therese of Lisieux,* trans. F. J. Sheed, 1949, p. 303. Second citation p. 254.

Evil originates not in the absence of light, but in the effort to deny the darkness, in the smile that hides the hatred, in the tears and apparent hurt that mask the malice and fury. It requires great effort and commitment to truth to identify the locus of the lie. Unique Self teacher Martin Buber reminds us that evil "plays an uncanny game of hide-and-seek in the obscurity of the soul, in which it, the single human soul, avoids itself and hides."[11] It hides both from itself and from others. The primary method and motive of evil is disguise, which happens through denial, deception, and demonization.

All of the above are different ways to distort Self and Story. The individual, when ego is clarified and Unique Self realized, becomes an organ of experience for the whole Uni-verse. *Every human being has an infinitely dignified and worthy story that needs to be lived and loved and deserves to be told.* Every human also has a Unique Story to tell. That is what it means to be a Unique Self. That is what it means to be a lover. That is what it means to love God. And remember: The God you do not believe in does not exist.

To love God is to allow God to see with your eyes, to uniquely see what can be seen from your perspective with your unique depth and unique qualities. Self-love is to know your own nature, to perceive your Unique Self. Self-love is enlightenment. The nature of the Uni-verse is that it evolves. Life-forms differentiate from earlier life-forms and evolve in an ever-increasing order of complexity and consciousness. We know that complexity and consciousness are intimately related. They are the inside and outside of the same evolutionary unfolding.

The more complex the physical organism, the more evolved are the inner workings of consciousness of that same being. A rabbit is more materially complex and more conscious than a snail. A human being is more materially complex and conscious than a dog. While it may be true that a dog has Buddha nature, the dog will never know it. *Each original form provides original Being with*

---

11 Martin Buber, *Good and Evil* (New York: Charles Scribner and Sons, 1953), 111.

a unique experience of itself. An amoeba serves the divine with a particular experience of itself, a butterfly with another, a fish with yet another. A bird and a horse each provide yet another experience in which the divine experiences itself. The human being, however, is a quantum leap forward in consciousness. The human being is conscious and self-reflective. *In a complete human being, the Universe experiences itself completely.* To love is to see through God's eyes. This requires you to shift perspectives from that of your separate-self ego to your infinitely expansive Unique Self. To love God is to let God see through your eyes. The truth of love is that you can only love God or another through your eyes—which are the eyes of God. It is this very realization that obligates you to cleanse your doors of perception—the way God sees through your eyes— and open the gates of divine love. You see with and as the eyes of God only if you purify the pettiness of small self and uncoil the self-contraction of ego. It is only thus that God can see through the prism of your Unique Eyes. That is why you are obligated to clarify your perception. Any lack of wholeness on your part defaces the divine. Any blurriness in your Unique Perspective and perception obstructs the vision of God. If you cannot see clearly, you blind God:

> *If you are bland and blend,*
> *Tyrannized by the trend,*
> *The God mind*
> *Goes blind.*

All of this is by way of introduction to our core topic: the distinction between two models of evolutionary mysticism and why that distinction matters. We now turn to the core of our conversation.

Authentic and Unique Self Models Considered

The implicit assumptions of both the Unique and Authentic Self models of self, as articulated in *Your Unique Self* (2012) and *Evolutionary Spirituality* by Andrew Cohen (2011) respectively, suggest both a shared worldview and subtle but important distinctions in their vision of the ideal homo religious. These distinctions are foundational with vast implications in virtually every dimension of life, and therefore, they need to be laid out with clarity and precision. Each suggests a different understanding of what it means to wake up from the narrow identity as a separate self or ego self into a more enlightened and correct identity as, respectively, Authentic or Unique Self.

The former is often associated with what has come to be termed Evolutionary spirituality, and the latter is one of the first principles of what has come to be termed World Spirituality based on Integral principles. These terms are, however, confusing, as World Spirituality has a strong evolutionary dimension, and evolutionary spirituality has a strong world orientation. Both are also based on Integral principles. There are many distinctions between them, but both are important and legitimate faces of an Integral spirituality.

Both the Unique Self and Authentic Self models locate themselves within the context of classical mystical enlightenment teaching. Neither emerges from a western flatland paradigm which views the self as an isolated and discrete unit, or what has been called a skin-encapsulated ego. For both Unique Self and Authentic Self, the first major step towards enlightenment is the realization that the person is not merely an ego or separate self, but rather that the person's true identity is their absolute, essential, or True Self.

In this movement, which is a result of practice, orientation, and occasionally grace, the mistaken identity of separateness is overcome once the person realizes that she is indivisible from and identical with the seamless coat of the universe. In the language of one Hindu mystic, "God appears in you as you." Your true identity, known by many names, but having no name, is the underlying Eros of Spirit, Buddha nature, *Ayin*, Tao, the Atman which is Brahman, or Essence which is beneath and beyond your felt sense of separation. This classical enlightenment teaching, what I shall refer to as True Self enlightenment, has two major qualities. The first quality is its eternal nature. To wake up to True Self is to access in first person the eternal principle of essence that lives as you and to identify with that principle as your essential identity, rather than with your small and contracted separate self. Your ego self is understood to be a contraction of your essential eternal self.[12]

The second quality of your True Self is its impersonal nature. It lives in precisely the same way in every person. It is beyond the personal, and the personal is classically realized to be the realm of separation, contraction, and illusion—the primary cause of suffering. To awaken to your True Self, then, is to awaken to your essence or emptiness, depending on how one is telling the enlightenment story.[13] True Self enlightenment is to realize your essential self as a being that is eternal and impersonal.

Both the Unique Self and Authentic Self teachings incorporate classical True Self awakening as core to their model. The clarion call of the Authentic Self model, however, is in virtually every publication both in print and online—evolution beyond ego. Courses abound in the principles for evolution beyond ego. In Unique Self teaching, there is a different orientation that expresses itself, not by stamping out the ego, but by recognizing its place in the evolutionary goal for humanity. In other words, ego is not only a contraction of the vastness, as the Eastern spiritual traditions correctly point out. Ego is a crucial step on the road to Unique Self. We never leave the ego behind. Rather, we trance-end our exclusive identification with ego. I have formulated this in teaching for many years in some version of the sentence, "Never evolve beyond ego, evolve beyond the exclusive identification with ego." Or alternatively, "The ego self is not a mistaken identity, but a limited identity." Also, "Clearly separate self exists in the mind of God, so to deny its reality is some mixture of heresy and psychosis." Some of the more evolved Western mystical traditions explicitly understood this; most did not. This understanding is virtually unknown in most popularly presented versions of eastern religion—some strains of Kashmir Shaivism, when correctly interpreted, offering a notable

---

12 It is true that the confusion between ego and Unique Self is still rampant in the world. See Gafni (2012) for "Twenty-Five Distinctions Between Ego and Unique Self," Chapter 6, pages 71-84.

13 See Ives (1995) for more on this point.

exception. This realization on a global scale is the precise next step in our evolution.

However, they both also share the core intuition that True Self, the realization of classical enlightenment in which one becomes identified with one's true nature beyond the Separate Self, is a critical step along, but not the endgame of, the enlightenment path. In the Authentic Self model, enlightenment comes to mean identifying your true nature as that which is eternal, evolutionary, and impersonal. In the Unique Self model, enlightenment comes to mean identifying your true nature as that which is eternal, evolutionary, and radically personal. Both models are emerging as mainstream forces in the post-postmodern restructuring of identity.

This overview brings us closer to the key issue of this book. Within the Integral reconstructive project, there have been two essential updates of enlightenment teaching. Both the Authentic Self and Unique Self enlightenment teachers share the first update, while hotly contesting the second. Both updates are rooted in a deeper understanding of the world of form. In the classic enlightenment teaching articulated by the Buddhist master Nagarjuna, emptiness is form and form is emptiness. Emptiness—which is the depth ground of all being—never appears independently of form. Form is the manifest expression of reality. In the world of form, as it relates to enlightenment, there are two primary emergent understandings which are critical to the evolution of enlightenment itself. The first update, shared and incorporated by both models, is the pivotal recognition that the world is evolving. Consciously aligning with the ceaselessly creative impulse of the cosmos, what has been termed the "evolutionary impulse" and that which is core to what has been termed "conscious evolution," is critical in both models.[1] Until the first decades of the twentieth century, the generally accepted scientific truth was that the world was eternal and unchanging. With the twentieth century comes the new realization that all of manifest reality in all of its expressions is, in its core nature, evolutionary. Unique Self teaching has as one of its pivots a teaching referred to as the "five big bangs."[14] Authentic Self and

---

14 Five big bangs, here, is a term adapted from Rolston (2010). He identifies

Unique Self teaching concur in their core reading of the first four big bangs. However, Unique Self teaching discerns a fifth big bang, which is explicitly and implicitly denied or ignored by Authentic Self teaching.

Stated succinctly: Each big bang is marked by a momentous leap of emergence.

Manifest reality was birthed and set into motion by the first big bang or what Brian Swimme, emerging out of Thomas Berry's teaching, has called the great flaring forth.[15] This initiated what we now can refer to as cosmological evolution. The second big bang, again a momentous leap of emergence or great flaring forth, is when matter awakens as life. Already in the 19th century, the new awareness of biological evolution swept the world. Matter awakened to life, drawn forward by the strange attractors of evolutionary Eros.

The second big bang initiated biological evolution. In the late 17th and 18th centuries, a growing awareness of the third big bang, a momentous leap of emergence, a great flaring forth, cultural evolution, began to make itself known. Between fifty to two hundred thousand years ago, primates began to wake up in an entirely new and emergent way, and what we know of as human cultural evolution began to develop. Culture goes through a series of structure stages of development, discernible across many lines of growth, including interior, exterior, communal, and collective streams—from the cognitive to the communal, technological, psychological, spiritual, and more. Some time in the last several hundred years, what may be termed the fourth big bang, a

three cultural big bangs of matter-energy, life, and mind. M. Gafni (AYUS, week 2, 2013) identifies five big bangs related to Unique Self that expand on Rolston: cosmological, biological, cultural, evolution awakening to itself, and evolution awakening to itself catalyzed by your Unique Self.
(Week 2 of *Awakening Your Unique Self* (2013). Available http://uniqueself. com/unique-self-courses/)
15 Swimme, B. (1994). The universe story: From the primordial flaring forth to the Ecozoic era—A celebration of the unfolding of the cosmos. New York: HarperOne Reprint Edition.

momentous leap of emergence, a great flaring forth, erupted, and evolution awakened to itself through human consciousness. For the first time, the human being was conscious of the evolutionary process. In Julian Huxley's famous phrase, evolution begins to awaken to itself through human awareness. Evolution awakens to itself most clearly through what my colleague Andrew Cohen has termed Authentic Self and what some of his students have termed Evolutionary Self.

Finally, what I have termed the fifth the big bang exploded. It is here that Unique Self realization goes beyond Authentic Self understanding. This fifth momentous leap of emergence, this great flaring forth, is expressed as the unique human being becoming aware that his and her own irreducibly unique development as irreducible expressions of the initiating love intelligence of all-that-is, and this awakening impulse is a core drive of the evolutionary process. The human being awakens not only as Authentic Self or Evolutionary Self, but as Evolutionary Unique Self. A full 13.7 billions years of evolution produce an irreducibly unique human being, and becoming that has the developmental capacity to consciously align the individual with the ecstatic evolutionary impulse. What Charles Pierce originally termed Evolutionary Love, the initiating and animating Eros of reality, awakens uniquely through the human being. Uniqueness—emergent from the Unique Self teaching—is understood to be not a function of contraction, but a quality of Essence. Evolution, or what we might call Love-in-Action or Spirit-in-Action awakens as the human being realizes that he or she is an irreducibly unique expression of the love intelligence and love beauty that is the initiating, driving, and animating Eros of all of reality. The process reveals its personal face. Evolution gets personal as the human being awakens to the realization that he or she is the personal face of Essence, the irreducibly unique expression of Love-in-Action.

After four great cycles of evolution, cosmological, biological, cultural, and evolutionary self-awakening, the fifth big bang is evolution's awakening to its personal dimension. The process reveals its personal face. The self awakens as evolution itself, realizing that her or his awakening is in effect the evolution of the manifest God. Not only does evolution wake up to itself through humanity, evolution wakes up as your Evolutionary Unique Self.

Today, I am what I call dual citizen of World Spirituality and Hebrew Wisdom. A major dimension of these core teachings comes to me via the lineage of Kabbalah, the Hebrew mystical teaching, which is my original lineage home.[16] I will cite in the main text here two passages from only one one thinker, a thinker who reflects this larger strain, which I have termed Evolutionary Kabbalah and which many scholars, including the likes of Huston Smith, have entirely missed in their presentations of Judaism.

A Kabbalistic Teaching on Evolution
By Abraham Kook, Lights of Holiness, Translated by M. Gafni.

> The theory of evolution, which is presently conquering the world, is aligned with the most profound secrets of the Kabbalah, more than any other philosophical theories.
>
> Evolution, which proceeds on an ascending trajectory, provides an optimistic base for the world, for how is it possible to despair when one sees that everything is evolving and ascending?
>
> And when we penetrate the very center of the principle of ascending evolution, we discover that it is the divine principle, which is enlightened with absolute clarity. For it is Infinity in realization that realized itself through bringing infinity from infinite potentiality to infinite actuality {infinitely}.
>
> Evolution enlightens all dimensions of reality, all of God's manifestations.

---

16 For extensive primary sources on the Evolution of God being the primary role of the fully awakened person, see the tab "Evolutionary Kabbalah" on marcgafni.com, where a dozen major sources are adduced in full and translated into English. This has been a major feature of my teaching, emergent from kabbalaistic sources for over twenty-five years. See, for example, Marc Gafni, *Soul Prints* (2001) part 1, for the teaching "Charity saves God from death." Abraham Joshua Heschel (1976) refers to this teaching as Divine Pathos, and more classical scholars, such as Moshe Idel (1990), refer to it as theurgy.

All of reality evolves and ascends, as is evident in its parts,
And this ascension is general as well as particular.
It rises to the highest peaks of absolute good.
It is self-evident that good and the whole are interrelated,
And reality is prepared to attain this quality, in which the All absorbs all of the good in all its parts.
This is the general ascending, in which all particular parts participate.
No spark is lost from the binding of unity; all are ready for the Great Feast.
To attain this goal the spirit must aspire to sublime divine passion, which is formed by faith-inspired work with God.

For Kook, the evolutionary principle is the essential texture of Kabbalah. The evolution of the part is part of the evolution of the whole. The Whole—the love intelligence that animates All-That-Is or God—is in a constant state of evolutionary development. Perfection itself is constantly perfecting. Kook amplifies these ideas in a second text.

Two Types of Perfection
By R. Kook, Translated by M. Gafni.

We perceive there to be two types of Perfection in absolute divine Perfection: One type of Perfection is so great and complete that no additional evolution is relevant to it.

If, however, there were no possibility of additional evolving whatsoever, this in and of itself would be an imperfection. For Perfection that is constantly waxing greater has great advantage and is pleasurable and is uplifting.

For we yearn for it exceedingly, proceeding from strength to strength. Divine Perfection can therefore not be lacking the dimension of perfecting which is the evolving process of perfecting and unfolding power.

This is why divinity has the ability to be creative, to instigate limitless cosmic be-ing and becoming, proceeding through all its levels and stages and growing.

It therefore follows that the essential divine soul of being, that which gives it life, is its constant ascending. That is its divine foundation, which calls it to be and to evolve.

The more science bases itself on evolution, the more it approaches the highest divine enlightenment, and the more it touches the most sublime of visions.

For the entirety of being cannot be judged by its partial relativity, that is to say, by means of the relation between one part and another, for this will not lead us to its true nature.

In truth, its primary inner law is the general relation of its entirety and all of its parts to divine wholeness.

This is the most eminent of all and the most worthy principle upon which to understand the foundation of all of reality.

These are radical teachings, expressing the evolutionary cast of Hebrew mysticism. It is worth noting that the word "evolution" is not my overlay on Kook's teaching. Rather, Kook used the modern Hebrew word for "evolution," with all of its modern implications. According to Unique Self mystic Abraham Kook, by consciously aligning yourself with the evolutionary principle, your "entire existence is divinely transformed and exalted." This is core to the Unique Self model.[17] Some version of this new evolutionary universe story is essential to the Integral reconstructive project. The version that is being adopted today in Integral circles, however, would benefit importantly from the more personally valenced realization that uniquely characterizes the kabbalistic lineage's teaching on evolutionary awakening. It seems worthwhile, therefore, to devote several paragraphs to getting a conceptual taste of kabbalistic realization of evolutionary consciousness so that it's fragrance can begin to perfume the broader evolutionary spirituality conversation. Before proceeding, it is of course worth noting that the kabbalists did not talk overtly about biological evolution, which only came to play in Darwin's time. They were

---

17 See chapter 4, 8, and 9 in *Your Unique Self.*

of course also not talking about physical cosmological evolution which only emerged as reality in twentieth century. Rather, the kabbalists assumed that all of reality evolved as a meta-principle but their actual realization of evolution was particularly in regard to the evolutionary impact of an individual's ethical and spiritual evolution on the evolution of the whole.

For Kook, the evolution of the part is part of the evolution of the whole. The whole—the love intelligence that animates All-That-Is, God—is in a constant state of evolutionary development. Perfection itself is constantly perfecting. According to Unique Self mystic Abraham Kook, by consciously aligning yourself with the evolutionary principle, your "entire existence is divinely transformed and exalted." In Kook's non-dual realization, the personal is the evolutionary. Personal evolution affects cosmic evolution.

We do not need to subscribe to the old biblical worldview of a God, merely separate from reality, guiding it from without, in order to recognize the radical intelligence that animates reality. As my colleague Ken Wilber and many others have correctly pointed out, the idea that evolution is a random, chance unfolding, which is not internally animated by a living Eros and telos, is an absurdity. Statistically, this possibility is billions of times less likely than a monkey typing out *War and Peace.* Those are not odds you would want to stake anything on, let alone the very meaning of your life. All of our faculties of perception—the eye of the flesh, the eye of the mind, and the eye of the spirit— make this obvious to us. Let's now step deeper into the flavor of this kabbalistic evolutionary realization, what I have called the awakening to Evolutionary Unique Self.

Each stage of evolution needs to receive the core gifts of the earlier levels and offer its own Unique Gift. Human beings evolve through levels of consciousness until they become capable of reflecting on themselves and their True Nature. This reflection yields the awareness of evolution itself.

The awareness dawns that you are part of the divine whole evolving through you and you begin to realize that you have a choice, one dramatic choice, from which all else flows. *You can ignore your True Nature or you can realize your True Nature.* To realize your True Nature is to align yourself with God, who is revealed as not separate from the evolutionary impulse of the kosmos itself, surging through you as you reflect, choose, and act in the world. The kabbalists realized that God is much more than the ostensibly impersonal evolutionary impulse, but also affirmed that god is not less than evolutionary impulse.

To align yourself with the evolutionary impulse coursing through you is to wake up as evolution. You experience yourself beyond your level-one personal, which is the separate-self ego. You experience yourself as a personal and potent incarnation of the process. You identify fully with the awakened evolutionary creativity, living consciously and uniquely in you. In you, evolution awakens to itself. This is the evolutionary context of Unique Self.

Being, Becoming, and Unique Self

Being is evoked by beauty. The wonder of a flower, a gorgeous woman or man, and the ocean all evoke the quality of Being. This is why we love them so much. All of these expressions of divine love-beauty are understood by the great traditions as being one face of the divine feminine. What is particularly wondrous about these manifestations of love-beauty is that you do not need to be especially evolved or perceptive to be moved by them. A baby is of the same ilk. The baby evokes Being. The value of a baby is wholly independent of any process of Becoming. This is why we are entranced by babies, beauty, and roses for their own sake. We do not gaze at the ocean, a beautiful woman or man, a rose, or a baby in order to advance some noble goal. Rather, we delight in gazing at them purely for the sake of the pleasure we derive from looking. Indeed, not only are these experienced without the goal of gaining position in the world of Becoming, the very opposite is true—the reward offered by the world for success in Becoming is the delight of Being. Sensual beauty and delight, from the gorgeous partner to the oceanfront home, have long been the rewards of successful Becoming.

Becoming is evoked by the joy of achievement. It involves effort, and it is directional—always moving toward a new goal. It delights in working hard and views walks in the park with suspicion. *For those seeking the ecstasy of Becoming, it matters not so much what is achieved. The fact of becoming itself brings joy in its wake.* The masculine is more drawn to Becoming, while the feminine is more drawn to the radiance of Being. The masculine gets together in a group in order to do something. The feminine will more readily get together purely for the joy of being together.

Being requires Becoming. It is the quality of Becoming that moves us to build hospitals, make revolutions, and evolve our scientific knowledge of the kosmos. All medicine is a child of Becoming. Without Becoming, Being might become lethargic and comatose, and the evolution of consciousness and love might never take place.

Becoming requires Being. It is Being that allows the Unique Self to engage the world passionately, even as it is not attached to the fruits of its labor. It is connection between Being and Becoming that lies at the core of the *Upanishads'* prescription for living: *Action in inaction. Inaction in action.* Both Being and Becoming are qualities of the Unique Self. In the evolutionary mysticism of the Hebrew sages, in radical departure from Aristotle, Being is infinitely inferior to Becoming. Even God, to be perfect—argued the mystics—must be Becoming. Which person do we think of as more evolved: one who is static or one who is always growing and expanding?

Clearly the latter, respond the mystics to their own question. A person who is not growing is in some sense flawed. Some would even say that the moment we stop growing, we start to die. Well then—why would you deny God the same perfection?

"Know yourself" is the Unique Self maxim of the Delphic Oracle. But we must not forget Oscar Wilde's remark: "Only the shallow know themselves." There is much more to you than you are presently aware of. When you give up your commitment to the next moment's unfolding, you give up on God, on your divinely unfolding Unique

Self. The essence of every moment, wrote philosopher Alfred North Whitehead, is "the creative advance into novelty." Every moment contains a new invitation for the evolutionary creativity of self becoming and personal transformation. God's gift to you is your life. Your unfolding and growth during that life is your gift back to God, for God expands in your growth.

YOUR EVOLUTIONARY YES

Your divine spark manifests as your drive to attain something beyond the contracted self of ego. You do not simply want to *disappear* into the one. Rather, your internal drive is to *appear* as a unique *expression* of the One. It is the answer to the question you are constantly asking: "Who am I?"

In the daily practice of Kabbalah, the seeker goes back to the moment before the world was created, to when the divine spark initiated the evolutionary process. This moment is available right now. You were there at the very beginning. *Hitboddedut* is the name of one of many forms of meditation designed to get you there. You enter deeply into the center of your being until everything but that center falls away. It is the Ground of Being—*ayin* or absolute nothingness—that is paradoxically personal and knows your name. Holy paradox lives in this realization.

The God train to this face of being is certain kinds of meditation and certain forms of chant. You rest in the timeless time and placeless place. In the language of Solomon, "His left hand is under my head, his right hand embraces me." You feel the divine embrace. No matter where or how you fall, you fall into the hands of God. This is the ground. Even when everything falls away, you are still there. When you awaken in the morning, the first practice you do is to contact this ground and realize your presence in it and as it. It is about this ground that we speak when we speak of the One, the unified ground of reality that is always and already you. Even as it personally holds you.

Once you realize this identification, your relation with all of reality is transformed. You have left the narrow straits of Egypt and have started to walk in the wide places. You have accessed the truth of your wider self. You have discovered Big Mind, Big Heart, Original Face, All-That-Is, Essence—all names for what lies right beneath your personality. It is the *ayin* before the *yesh*, the unmanifest ground from which all that is manifest is born. In this place you taste, for the first time, your freedom. One Taste.

The moment when *ayin* reveals itself as *yesh*, when the peace-bliss of an unchanging God explodes with a big bang as dynamic and evolving divinity who is movement and direction itself, is called the Mystery of Creation. That which is perfect seeks an even higher perfection, as if such words could be spoken or understood. *The changeless, motivated by infinite ecstatic love, suffers the exquisite pain of change and evolutionary revelation in order to give gifts of love that would otherwise remain un-given. And un-given love is not love.* The Second Taste. All reality emerges from what is called by the kabbalists *nekudah achat*, a single point. In that single point, you are there. At that moment, from the depth of that point, you decided to unfurl a world. You, God, created the Uni-verse. It was not your ego, but your Unique Divine Essence that made the mysterious choice to create a world. It was your Unique Self that initiated the big bang. The purpose was simple and clear—for the higher good of all sentient beings.

At the moment of the big bang, the original light of infinite goodness is shattered. It is shattered in the way that the heart of the lover is shattered: by opening in love to the beloved. It is shattered by an infinite desire to move from Being to Becoming; to merge with the beloved, and through that merger, to emerge into greater Being. It is to be more glorious, more beautiful, more awake, and more in love than was ever possible before.

Infinity and unity explode into finite, disconnected shards of the original divine unity. The process of evolution begins. Slowly the light hidden in the dark shards of the broken vessels is re-gathered. Divinity is rebuilt through first-, second-, and third person reconstructive projects. *Buddha* is the first-person project of meditation and introspection. *Sangha* is the second-person project of social artistry and transformation coupled with prayer, chant, and devotion to the beloved. *Sangha* is always with thou and with the Thou of God. *Dharma* is the third-person project of developing discernment and right understanding, and therefore, right action in the world.

This whole impersonal process of evolution is all very personal. It speaks directly to you. You feel it inside of you right now as the powerful desire to awaken and be more. That desire is God desiring to be more through and as you. *When you enter into your deepest self, you begin to clarify your desire.* You realize with absolute shock, joy, and delight that God not only desires but needs your Becoming. It is this realization that we call the New Enlightenment of Unique Self.

Evolution—
Personal and Impersonal Dimensions

Unique Self demands that you see your entire life, everything that you live, breathe, feel, think, or desire, on all levels of your Being, within the larger framework of your direct participation in the evolution of God. It is this larger context that is the key to your liberation. The Unique Self mystics have taught for over a thousand years that every human action should be preceded by an affirmative statement of meaning: "I do this act for the sake of unifying and evolving divinity."[18] When every significant action you take is for the sake of the all, infused with a profound awareness of your evolutionary context, you stop reacting from ego and begin acting from the place of a powerful evolutionary integrity.

Renaissance kabbalist Isaac Luria developed a highly elaborate series of *kavvanot,* intentions. Each was a formal affirmation said at a different moment during the day, in order to awaken and align the intention of the individual with the evolutionary divine context in which he or she lived and breathed. For Isaac Luria, arguably the

---

18 The precise Hebrew word used is "Yichud," which in many texts is deployed in a virtually identical manner to the term "*tikkun.*" *Tikkun,* as I discuss elsewhere, is often translated as "to evolve."

most significant kabbalist of the last thousand years, the ecstatic human obligation to awaken to Unique Self is the primary source of joy. It is the giving of your Unique Gift that fills your life with direction, meaning, and delight.

The split between the personal and the impersonal disappears as you awaken to your unique *tikkun* (fixing) in the larger context of the field of all life that ever was, is, and will be. It is for this reason that there is little talk in the Kabbalah about individual enlightenment. The danger of excessive emphasis on the individual is that you become a spiritual narcissist, totally focused on your experience of freedom and spaciousness. You then confuse that with Liberation, which it is not. *Enlightenment is an embodied activist relation to reality infused with evolutionary integrity, which is far beyond the awakening of True Self.*

Ken Wilber, drawing not at all from Kabbalah, but from De Chardin, Pierce, Aurobindo, the earlier German idealists of the 19th century,[2] and a host of other earlier sources, makes the evolutionary teaching central to the Integral reconstructive project. For anyone who truly understands Integral theory, the word "integral" and the word "evolutionary" are at least somewhat redundant.[19] For Integral theory to awaken comes to mean not only awakening to the eternal and unchanging True Self, which is the ground of being, but also awakening to what Barbara Marx Hubbard and others termed the evolutionary impulse[20] of emergence, which is

---

19 Ken Wilber has championed the vision of an evolving enlightenment. I have spent hours talking to Ken Wilber and Michael Murphy in separate conversations about the nature of their awakening to the evolutionary realization. Ken cut his teeth—to borrow his term—with the perennial philosophers, who were the dominant voice in the L.A. Vedanta Society. At some point, however, Ken broke with them and embraced the evolutionary view, bringing his pandit vision to the deepening and evolving of that very view in a number of critical ways.

20 See for example Hubbard, *Conscious Evolution*, New World Library, 1997, p. 69. There may be earlier usages of this term which Hubbard was drawing from in Gerard Heard and others, but I have not traced the intellectual history of the term. It is a project worth doing.

This teaching, partially sourced in Kabbalah, had direct influence on the German idealists Fichte and Schelling. (Kabbalah scholar Eliot Wolfson (2005) has already pointed to a vast literature showing the kabbalistic influence via

the ground of becoming. The evolutionary matrix is as we have seen just now similarly central to the kabbalistic framework, which is one of the key sources for the evolutionary emergent of the Unique Self teaching. My lineage teacher Abraham Kook spoke for the kabbalistic tradition on the issue of the evolutionary nature of spirit and all of reality. At the same time the difference between the personal quality of the evolutionary awakening through the prism of Unique Self and the impersonal quality of evolutionary awakening in evolutionary spirituality is significant and as we shall see, has profound implications.

At this point, allow me to enter this evolutionary spirituality conversation more personally and say something about my sources. I am an evolutionary mystic. I come from a tradition of evolutionary mystics. My lineage masters in Kabbalah, whose transmission I received, understood and clearly articulated that the specific privilege and wild responsibility of the human being is to awaken to conscious evolution. And these very evolutionary mystics comprise one dimension of the original inspiration for the core teaching of Unique Self, the evolutionary dimension. The second source for the Unique Self teaching was my own awakening to the infinity of intimacy, the quality of which is absolutely personal. This realization found deep resonances in the esoteric sources of Hebrew mysticism.[21]

The full human awakening to enlightened consciousness, which needs to be redone everyday, is the awakening to Evolutionary Unique Self. The awakening to what I have called

---

key Renaissance writers and other key channels on Fichte and Schelling.) See also the related endnotes on Wolfson and evolutionary Kabbalah at the end of this document.

21 My doctoral dissertation (Radical Kabbalah, Vol. 1 and Vol. 2, Integral Publishers, 2011) spends some thousand pages unpacking the core lineage sources which hold the enlightened eros of Unique Self as the penultimate model of enlightenment. These sources rooted in the earliest hebraic texts run from the biblical and Talmudic matrix into a rich vein of thousands of esoteric texts which find their way from the Zohar, through Luria and into hassidism and ultimately to the very same Abraham Kuk. It is from them merged with my own personal graced realization that I was able to articulate a vison first of Unique Self and then of Evolutionary Unique Self.

Evolutionary Unique Self is described (in pre-modern terms) by mystic Isaac Luria. Kabbalah scholar M. Kallus characterizes the Lurianic realization as being absolutely non-dual, one in which the human being awakens to his or her place as a unique and personal incarnation of the divine process. This creates an activist posture in which human consciousness is realized to be an expression of evolving divine consciousness. This activist posture, based on the evolutionary impulse living personally in the human being, caused Kallus to characterize Luria's mysticism with the poignant pathos of Nikos Kazantzakis' phrase, "We are the saviors of God."

For Kook, drawing on Luria, waking up as evolution, as Unique Self, as evolutionary Unique Self, and becoming the "savior of god" was the core spiritual imperative of the kabbalist. The evolutionary cast of kabbalistic ideas has remained obscure even to both mainstream kabbalists and mainstream Kabbalah scholars, with some notable exceptions. Only a very select few have written on the kabbalistic sources of Evolutionary teaching,[22] and fewer still have noticed the striking resonance between Kook's writings to those of Aurobindo, the other great evolutionary mystic of the 20th century.[23]

Levels of the Personal

In the Integral world, effective practices and original, powerful articulations of the impersonal evolutionary teaching have been developed in a sustained fashion in the Authentic Self model. Much as the Unique Self model has evolved the thinking of many teachers, so has the thinking of the Authentic Self model. Mutual exchange and influence between schools of thought that are proximate in time and space with overlapping agendas is a key methodology of the evolutionary impulse.[24]

However, as we have pointed out, *there's a second evolution of*

---

22 See Ben Shlomo, pp. 289-309. See also the "Evolutionary Kabbalah" tab at marcgafni.com and chapters 8 & 9 in *Your Unique Self* for more on evolutionary spirituality.
23 See related endnote in this book.
24 Johnson, S. (2010). *Where good ideas come from: The natural history of innovation.* Riverhead.

the enlightenment teachings, which like the new evolutionary insight similarly derives from emergent insights about the nature of the world of form. This is a re-evaluation and significant upgrade of the value of the personal. Just like we realize that the world of form is evolving, we also realize that the world of form is becoming more and more individuated as we evolve to higher and higher levels of consciousness. This individuation, however, is not an expression of separateness or alienation. Quite the opposite. It is an expression of essence individuating in personal forms, all of which form a higher seamless integration. I have spent much of the last twenty years unfolding and evolving this core teaching that I have called Unique Self in a series of both academic and spiritual publications and teaching frameworks.[25]

One of the areas where modernity and postmodernity provided a key evolutionary update to spirit was in regard to the notion of personal self. Older strains of spiritual thought, including the notion of *homo imago dei* in the biblical book of Genesis, were evolved, stripped of their ethnocentric context, and placed front and center in society in the Renaissance when the word "self" first appeared in the dictionary.[26] Prior to the Renaissance, the self was defined primarily by roles.[27] In the Renaissance, the self became an autonomous and self-justifying unity independent of larger contexts. The renaissance brought the idea and experience of personal perspective front and center. With self, perspective comes online, and that perspective is absolutely personal. Perspective can pathologize by disassociating from the larger context, or perspective can individuate the larger context. From an enlightenment perspective—which sees the larger context as the ground of being itself, True Self—the following two equations express both possible results from the emergence of perspective. Personal perspective -

---

25   For a complete intellectual history of Unique Self as Marc Gafni has developed it since 1989, please view the timeline available at http://uniqueself. com/unique-self-timeline/.

26   On the emergence of "self" in the Renaissance dictionary, see for example, A. Storr (2005) and C. Taylor (1989).

27   See, for example, K. Wilber's (1981) discussion of the emergence of self in *Up From Eden*.

True Self = separate self or ego self. Or alternatively, True Self + personal perspective = Unique Self.[28] This latter equation, core to the Unique Self model, expresses the personal, post-emptiness, post-realization, which has been cleansed of the distortions of the personal pre-realization.[29]

To state it succinctly: The first emergence of the personal comes after the pre-personal stage. I refer to this as level-one personal. Level-one personal is the level of separate self, personality, and ego. From one perspective, this is utterly necessary to form a healthy human identity. Ego is understood as the organizing principle in the identity of the separate self. However, this identity is limited. To awaken into enlightenment, one needs to move beyond the exclusive identification with ego self. The ego identification of level-one personal creates a contracted human identity, which the classical enlightenment teachers correctly pointed to as the source of suffering. One must transcend level-one personal into the impersonal ground of being, which is one's True Self. It is impersonal in the sense of being beyond level-one personal—in other words, beyond separate self, ego, and personality. This is

---

28   For the history of the equation, emergent from dialogues with Ken Wilber from 2003-2005 see in fn. 27, in the footnotes to Chapter 2 & 3 in *Your Unique Self* (2012). I had brought to the table the unique perspective of True Self which in the legal mysticism of Talmudic discourse was the source of the creation of "New God" or said differently "New Torah," which Ken then formulated as True Self + perspective = Unique Self. The actual correspondence around these issues from those dialogues is reproduced in the footnotes cited.

29   Ken Wilber, in *Sex, Ecology, Spirituality* (1995), develops the "personal-plus," "personal-minus" distinction, which is a step in the direction of Unique Self. It asserts that what I have termed level-one personal, the personal before the realization of True Self, does not disappear with the appearance of True Self. However, this formula does not yet intuit the personal beyond the impersonal. This is the province of Unique Self, which Ken and I formulated, and clarified and evolved jointly in a series of pivotal dialogues, about a decade after the release of *SES*. Ken has termed Unique Self a new chapter in Integral theory. See Ken Wilber, preface to *Re-reading ritual: On the evolution of tears, first steps towards Integrally informed religion—The model of Rosh Hashanah* (Integral Publishers, 2014) See also Sean Esbjörn-Hargens, Executive Editor, *JITP*, 6:1, "The evolutionary emergent of Unique Self: A new chapter in Integral theory," Marc Gafni, SUNY Press, 2010.

what many enlightenment teachers refer to when they talk about the Impersonal. That, however, is not the end of the personal. The personal is a core quality of essence. When we talk of someone touching us personally, or the personal quality of a connection, we are referring to a quality of unique intimacy. Essence is from one perspective the infinity of intimacy. Unique Self is the individuation of intimacy.[30] When a student asks me, Who am I?, I invariably respond, "You are God's unique intimacy." Beyond level-one personal is level-two personal or the higher personal which clarifies and reveals itself post-contact with some level of True Self. From a level-two personal perspective, we realize that although essence may be more than personal, it is never less than personal. This is the personal beyond the impersonal. This is one of the core realizations of Unique Self enlightenment. This is the unique individuation beyond ego, which is Unique Self enlightenment. This is the uniqueness beyond separateness, a distinction to which I devoted a full chapter of *Your Unique Self.*

So, in effect there are three core stations of consciousness described here. The first is personal, the second impersonal, and the third is personal yet again. This second appearance of the personal, which arises from the impersonal, is level-two personal, and forms the essence of what I have termed Unique Self. This teaching is rooted in kabbalistic lineage, which understands enlightenment as the awakening not only to *Ayin* or *sunyata,* the suchness that lives in you, but also as both the clarification and enactment of post-egoic uniqueness. Enlightenment is an awakening in this teaching, not only into the taste of undifferentiated being, but into unique being and becoming.[31] This model of enlightenment is activistic at its core and is what I have termed in other writings Non-Dual Humanism.[32]

---

30 See *Your Unique Self* (2012), chapter 1.
31 See M. Gafni, *Radical Kabbalah, Unique Self and Non Dual Humanism* (2012). Tucson, AZ: Integral Publishers.
32 Many kabbalistic scholars have missed this strain in Kabbalah. But, it is a critical strain, which I develop fully in a two-volume academic work entitled *Radical Kabbalah* (2012). See also longer endnote in this volume.

CHAPTER 2:

Ten Core Distinctions Between Unique Self and Authentic Self

It is the place of the personal in enlightenment teachings that is the great point of departure between Unique Self and Authentic Self, and it is various facets of this distinction as it has appeared in *Evolutionary Enlightenment: A New Path to Spiritual Awakening* (2011) and *Your Unique Self: The Radical Path to Personal Enlightenment* (2012), which the remainder of this essay will address.[3] I will unpack ten core distinctions between these models.

Before I cite a substantial set of passages illustrating the distinctions between the Unique Self and Authentic Self models and offer some brief commentary on them, I present here the set of equations that are explicit in the two core texts of these models, *Evolutionary Enlightenment* and *Your Unique Self.*

SET OF EQUATIONS:
AUTHENTIC SELF ENLIGHTENMENT MODEL

The Level of Personal Self

Ego = personal = separate self = individuated self sense = uniqueness = Unique Self sense = special = narcissist personality = inauthentic = merely personal = personal prism = secondary = external sheath = personal drama = petty personal = not you = personal which is "if not irrelevant, secondary" to process = personal which is "outer sheath" = relative = past = little or no choice = culturally conditioned = relative

The Level of Impersonal Self

Impersonal I = authentic self = evolutionary self = impersonal evolutionary impulse = impersonal process = absolute = truth of impersonality = impersonal creativity = primary = heroic impersonal = courageous = beyond ego = thrilling = future = Eros = Eros of evolutionary impulse = God = Eros of impersonal process = metaphor = no god outside of you = you = personal self is an illusion, result of conditioning = choice only at the level of the impersonal = impersonal process = god does not care about your personal self = god = metaphor for impersonal = god cares only about your contribution to the process = your personal needs are irrelevant or at least secondary to the process = you are not special= evolutionary we space

The entire book, *Evolutionary Enlightenment* shares the implications of this set of equations.

SET OF EQUATIONS:
UNIQUE SELF ENLIGHTENMENT MODEL

Unique Self Enlightenment includes both the impersonal {True Self} and the personal face of Essence, which is the personal that appears beyond the impersonal. The core distinction is between the personal that appears *before* the impersonal—that is, the so-called True Self—and the Personal that emerges *after* True Self has been realized, namely Unique Self:

> Evolutionary Emergent of Unique Self = Personal Face of Essence = Essence Beyond Ego = Distinction between personal at level of ego and Personal beyond True Self = Personal after Emptiness = there is no impersonal self anyplace in the manifest world = the impersonal is an illusion = the impersonal always appears personally in the manifest world = a person is special beyond ego = courageous = God having a You experience = uniqueness is an irreducible feather of essence = the personal beyond the impersonal = Self beyond Ego = individuation beyond Ego = Form and Emptiness are one = all four quadrants tetra arise = Individuation as Enlightenment = the post egoic personal face of the process = the unique post egoic personal incarnation of the evolutionary impulse = Unique Self = Eros of Unique Self = Eros = relationship = evolutionary intimacy = evolutionary we space= partnership with the divine = second face of god = uniqueness = choice fully emergent at the level of Unique Self = Self beyond Ego = New chapter in Integral Theory

The entire book *Your Unique Self* unpacks and explains the core implications of this series of equations.

THE SIX STATIONS OF UNIQUE SELF

Before proceeding it is important to outline, the basic trajectory of Unique Self enlightenment. There are six distinct stations in the evolution of identity on the path to your Unique Self. You will recognize them as you encounter them on your journey. I will now outline the stations to give you a view of the whole picture.

Station 1: Pre-personal Self

The first station appears at the beginning of life, before you have developed a sense of your personal separate self. In individual development, this is the station of the infant who is not yet individuated from their mother or environment. However, this pre-personal station doesn't disappear completely after infancy; it remains with us and reappears later in life in different forms.

It is, for example, the station of someone who loses their autonomy and sense of identity in an abusive cult or lynch mob or someone caught in the groupthink of politically correct victimology. Falling in love also requires you to move—at least for a time—from the clear boundaries of the personal to the fusion of the pre-personal. It is for this reason that Freud, in his less romantic moments, viewed falling in love as regressive. Deeper insight reveals that this "falling" is an absolutely necessary, if temporary, first station of love. It gives the lover a temporary glimpse into what might be possible. In the next station, boundaries snap back into place as the personal reasserts itself. This is the station where lovers must decide if they are willing to stay and do the work. If all goes well, you then evolve to station three, true love, when the infatuation of fusion is transmuted into the ecstasy of union. But the initial infatuation with another is one of the places, long after infancy, in which the pre-personal reappears in our lives.

Station 2: Separate Self: Level One Personal

In this station of development you move from the pre-personal to the first personal stage of human development. This is when the personality, sometimes referred to as the ego or separate self, comes online. The formation of personality and ego is a wonderfully healthy and necessary stage. You learn to experience yourself as a separate entity among many other separate entities, with your own boundaries and identity. The separate self is born. You feel joy at your success and frustration at your failure. At this station, the distinction between your false self, True Self, and Unique Self does not yet appear.

In this station you are wonderfully caught up in the glory of your story. In the best expression of this station, you are not thinking about your story; you are simply living it. There is great potential depth at this level of consciousness, expressed in part by a direct and unflinching recognition of what is. *There comes a time when, in order to grow, you need to get over the fantasy of your idealized life and start recognizing the story of your life for what it is.* You embrace your life in all of its complexity, ecstasy, and pain. You can bear it all, and you delight in it all, because it is your life. And in claiming your life as it is, you start to feel something deeply right about it and about yourself. There emerges in you a willingness to take absolute responsibility for everything that happens in your life. You are fully identified with your story. You are a player in your life and not a victim of its circumstances.

Many teachers like to say, "You are not your story." They are right, but only partially. They fail to distinguish between the ego story and the Unique Self story. But there is also great wisdom in this first level of the personal, the station of ego and personality. The ego *prefigures* the Unique Self. And as we shall see, there are many important stations through which you must still evolve toward your full depth and enlightenment. In the next stages of development, you will need to first clarify your story and then dis-identify with it in order to return to your ego story at a much higher level of consciousness, the level of Unique Self. While first glimmerings of Unique Self appear at this level of separate self, it can only fully be realized when ego gets over itself.

Station 3: False Self

False self is the unhealthy form of separate self. In this station, you take an essential step in the transformation and evolution of your identity. It is here that you begin to consciously deploy what Freud called the observing ego. Your ability to see the inner structure of your personality comes online. As you separate and look at the story of your life as an object, its contours and patterns begin to become clear to you. You begin to recognize some of the core beliefs that have defined and sometimes deformed your life.

Certain core mind-sets start to stand out. You see that you have a particular way of fixing your attention, of stabilizing yourself with familiar and deeply held beliefs.

In this station, the essential practice is that of "making subject object." Just as we get settled in the story of who we are, something amazing, something startling happens: We see that we have been telling a story. The entire narrative that we have formulated, the one that we have become so accustomed to, so comfortable with, slips from our subjective experience and becomes an object, an artifact. Remember Robert Kegan's insight: the subject of one level of development becomes the object of the next level of development. The understanding of this stage of the journey is based in part on the pioneering work of the great psychologists Robert Assagioli, Oscar Ichazo, and others, which reveals how the fixation of attention, which creates a false sense of self, is the very mechanism that prevents us from uncovering our deeper nature. Your fixation is the particular prism through which you see the world, the way in which, very early in your life, your attention fixated into a very particular pattern. This fixation of attention into a particular slant of seeing will naturally produce a distorted picture of your identity, which is your false self. Your false self is the unhealthy and distorted expression of your separate self.

Your false self fixation often expresses itself in a sentence or series of sentences: "I am not safe." "I am not enough." "I am bad." "I am too much." You live inside your sentence. *You need to step outside of your sentence in order to genuinely realize your True Self.* The model of the Enneagram type describes another kind of fixation. It is a distorted pattern of perceived meaning upon which you fixate early in your life, which then shapes and determines your experience of reality.

Recognizing these patterns, trance-ending them, and deploying them skillfully is the next critical step in your evolution. *To walk toward your enlightenment, you must recognize your fixations, break their hold on you, and cleanse the doors of your perception.*

To recognize your false self, you must first see it. This is the process of making subject—your false self—into object; your false self becomes an object that you can see and therefore change. The discernment of the observing ego allows you to take the first steps out of your false self into your real life. You still identify with your separate self, but without the distorting smoke and mirrors of your false self.

Station 4: True Self—Classical Enlightenment: Impersonal

In this station we make the momentous, freeing leap from the personal to the transpersonal. This has been called by some the liberation from the personal and the great realization of the impersonal. It would be more accurate to say that it is liberation from the ego personality, which is only level one of the personal. This level of the personal is transcended only to reappear in clarified form at the level of Unique Self. But first we must realize our True Selves.

We are ready and even yearning to evolve beyond our separate-self ego. We are no longer able to adhere to an identification with self that is painfully limited. The space beyond the story, the awareness beyond the fixations of attention, and the contracted conception of self now become the foreground instead of the background. This is the classical stage of ego dissolution. You realize your True Nature. Your identity shifts from your separate-self ego to your True Self. You move to trance-end your personality and identify with your essence. This is the change that changes everything.

Sometimes this dissolution occurs spontaneously, sometimes through overwhelming pain or extreme fatigue; at other times, it emerges as the fruition of years of dedicated study and practice. Yet even at this stage of development, the ego does not disappear. Rather the ego is freed from its own narcissism and becomes an ally. You never evolve beyond ego. You evolve beyond your exclusive identification with ego.

As you begin to dislodge from your exclusive identification with the separate self, as you become disillusioned, you may be fearful or anxious, longing for the old, solid ground of your narrow identity. At the same time, your growing sense is that you are part of an infinitely larger context, that you are part of the "seamless coat of the Uni-verse." Understand that this is not a one-time event, but a continuous process of death and rebirth at each and every moment. At this station, you engage in spiritual practice in order to dislodge your identity from the hell of separation, and you begin to realize your identity as the eternal Witness, as Big Mind/Big Heart, as the effortless spacious awareness behind this moment and every moment. You recognize your profound interconnectedness with others and the world. You realize that you are part of the larger field of love, intelligence, and creativity underlying All-That-Is. You reach beyond time and taste eternity, stepping out of the stream of past, present, and future, consenting to the full presence of the unchanging Now.

Two Notes on True Self

The first note concerns one's level of True Self realization and the relationship between True Self and Unique Self. Clearly there are different levels of True Self realization. Our evolution beyond exclusive identification with ego is an ongoing process, and it is fueled by regular practice. Many people have glimmerings of True Self realization at several different times in their lives and then remain faithful to the lived memory of that experience. (In fact, one definition of faith could be "living with fidelity to those moments when you authentically realize the true nature of your self and the universe"!)

All this means that levels of True Self realization vary greatly from person to person. It is fair to say, however, that there is a direct relationship between the level of your True Self realization and the clarity of your Unique Self awakening. The more deeply you know True Self, the more you can be sure that your experience of a distinctive self-sense is at the level of Unique Self and not merely the grasping of ego. The more experiences of True Self you have, especially if you ally them with certain practices (witness practice, surrender practice, and others), the more you are able to discern between the voices of your child-ego and the experience of self that comes from true alignment with the divine in you.

The second note concerns the nature and method of True Self realization. If you can only realize True Self by attaining the ultimate realization of Buddha, and if Unique Self comes online only after one has attained that level of True Self realization, then only a very few people could ever realize Unique Self. That would make Unique Self realization practically irrelevant for most human beings. Yet we know that True Self is accessed through many different means, not only through a non-dual realization, born of first-person meditative practice, as in the classical Zen *kensho* or Hindu *samadhi*.

Realizing True Self can happen through non-meditative experiences like prayer, ecstatic dance, spontaneous visionary experience, or even during a tennis game or a car accident. A sense of being enmeshed in and intertwined with invisible lines of connection that link all of reality may be accessed through direct contact with many forms of the transcendent, including contact with personal, second-person forms of the divine such as Christ or the divine mother. You can access glimmerings of True Self in the course of living for a higher social purpose or artistic vision, or by incarnating values like service and kindness. For example, my grandmother was a profoundly awake woman who experienced herself as selflessly committed to the highest good of all beings and connected to all beings. Her compassion was vast, and her consciousness was full of God-awareness. She never meditated or had a non-dual *satori* realization in her life. Indeed, she had never even heard of meditation. Her major formal spiritual practice was praying, reading psalms, and absorbing the laws and stories of the great Jewish masters, along with the ritual practices of Jewish teaching. All of this served to produce in her what can only be described as an enlightened consciousness, which had profoundly trance-ended separate self. There are many like her, who have had enough experience of contact with True Self to be able to awaken to their Unique Self, and to discern the difference between Unique Self and ego.

Doesn't unique self reveal itself before awakening?
Mozart?

Station 5: Unique Self—The New Enlightenment: Level Two Personal

At the fifth station you witness the emergence of Unique Self. The personal comes back online at a higher level of consciousness. You realize that your True Self is not merely an indistinct part of a larger unification, but expresses itself uniquely, and that you have a unique role to play in the evolutionary unfolding. *The personal face of your True Self is your Unique Self.* You are able to consciously incarnate the evolutionary impulse toward healing and transformation that initiates, animates, and guides reality.

No one else in the world can respond as you can to the unique need of *All-That-Is*, that is yours and only yours to address, and that is the place of your full liberation and power.

Awakening to your Unique Self has been called the "Pearl beyond Price" by the Sufi adherents, or *"ani* after *ayin"* by Kabbalists. It is alluded to as "Kosmic Consciousness assuming individual form" in the *Yoga Vasistha* of Hinduism.

Unique Self is not just another subtle disguise of the ego. Not in the least. Unique Self is rather the personal face of True Self. Unique Self is the antidote to the grasping of ego. In one moment you are fully alive, dynamically reaching for love and manifestation, and yet you are willing to let go of any attachment in the next moment. Your ego is still present, but you have moved beyond exclusive identification with your ego.

for kathnis its truth *for glory experience increase*

The ego points toward Unique Self. Your Unique Self, which begins to reveal itself at the level of personality, comes to full flower only after freeing itself from the grasping of ego through genuine and repeated experiences of ego clarification and trance-ending. Unique Self appears gradually and in direct proportion to the level of egoic clarification and trance-ending. Unique Self also shows up fleetingly in peak experiences in conjunction with parallel appearances of True Self. An example of this might be a moment of "flow" or an Eros experience, sometimes called "being in the zone," when ego temporarily drops, and a felt or even lived experience of Unique Self becomes temporarily available to the person.

In classical enlightenment, we move from an experience of ourselves as a-part, to a felt experience of ourselves as an indivisible expression of the larger oneness, where the sense of the part dissolves and the wholeness even momentarily overwhelms our sense of distinction. And then, in a subtle shift of emphasis, we evolve to an even deeper depth of realization. At this station, we begin to experience ourselves as the part again, but from the place of vast awareness, we realize that the part is not separate. We realize that we are not a separate but rather a unique part of a larger whole. And you realize that whole living in you, in part. *Your awakening or enlightenment has a perspective that is held only by you.*

True Self + Perspective = Unique Self

This stage is hinted at in the Tenth Oxherding picture in Buddhism, one of ten snapshots of enlightenment. In the tenth picture, the man walks back to the marketplace—and I would add "in order to offer his Unique Gifts and to perform the unique *bodhisattva* obligations that can and must be fulfilled by him alone."

Station Six: Evolutionary Unique Self

Personal and Impersonal:

It is not enough, however, to awaken only to your Unique Expression of True Self. As we will unfold in more depth in Chapter 8, there is a second critical dimension of awakening that is essential to Unique Self realization. I received a direct transmission of this second dimension of Unique Self enlightenment from my lineage teachers who are best described as evolutionary mystics.

Isaac Luria, the teacher of my teachers, the great evolutionary mystic of the Renaissance period, taught that every action that a person takes must be with the explicit consciousness and intention of *tikkun*. *Tikkun* is best translated as the evolutionary healing and transformation of all of reality.

Every action must be invested with evolutionary intention. In Luria's language, it must be *leshem yichud,* meaning for the sake of the evolutionary integration and transformation of all of reality.

Said simply in the language of the evolutionary mystics themselves, to awaken to your Unique Self is to "shift your perspective." The way the evolutionary mystics say it is simply to shift your perspective from "your side" to "God's side." To the evolutionary mystics, to awaken means not necessarily to have a profound mystical state experience in which you feel all of Being living in you; rather, to awaken is to dramatically, yet simply, shift.

From your side to the mysteries side

Station Six A: Unique Shadow

In the post-enlightenment experience, there are still layers to be shed. Even when we are most expansive, most identified with All-That-Is, small pockets of identity are kept out of our awareness, although they are experienced quite directly by everyone around us. You simply can't see them directly, even though recognizing them would free up your energy and directly facilitate a more powerful and beautiful expression of your Uniqueness. This is what is called, both in some of the great traditions and in modern psychology, your shadow.

Learning to recognize and do shadow work is one of the challenges of the full journey of Unique Self. Although shadow work begins at the level of separate self, the full completion of your shadow work is directly connected to your realization of Unique Self. The common understanding of shadow is the negative material about your self that you are unable to own in your first person. This negative material—your jealousy, pettiness, fear, rage, brutality—is understood to be generic. The same core material is said to show up and be repressed into shadow, to a greater and larger degree, by everyone.

This is a true but highly partial understanding of shadow. In Unique Self teaching, we evolve the shadow work conversation and realize that shadow is not generic—shadow is intensely personal. This is a critical evolutionary unfolding of our understanding of shadow.

Your personal shadow is your Unique Shadow. Your Unique Shadow is your dis-owned Unique Self, the unavoidable result of a life yet unlived. Shadow is not merely your repressed negative material. Shadow is your dis-owned, denied, or distorted Unique

Self. Your Unique Self and your Unique Shadow are a double helix of light and dark coiled into the patterns of becoming.

Remember William Blake's teaching on wisdom and folly: "If the fool would follow his folly, he would become wise." In precisely the same way, you can follow the path of your Unique Shadow back to your Unique Self. *You can almost learn more about yourself through your darkness than you can through your light.*

Station Six B: Your Unique Gift

The obligation that wells up from your evolutionary realization of Unique Self is your responsibility to give the gifts that are yours alone to give, gifts that are desired and needed by the rest of creation. Every human being has a particular set of gifts to offer in the world. Your Unique Perspective gives birth to what I call your Unique Gift.

The ability to offer this gift freely and fully depends on your ability to free yourself of limiting and false notions of who you are, and to instead identify with your larger service. And beautifully, when this happens you are also able to allow others to be fully who they are as Unique Beings: complete, whole, and specific. This is one of the litmus tests of whether you are in Unique Self or in ego, whether you are able to joyously recognize and affirm the Unique Self of others without feeling that they are taking something that is yours.

Your Unique Gift is the particular contribution that you can make to the evolution of consciousness, which can be made by no one else who ever was, is, or will be. Both the overwhelming desire and ability to give your Unique Gift is a direct and spontaneous expression of your Unique Self realization.

Your Unique Gift, whether public or private, is your divine evolutionary gift to All-That-Is. It is the very face of God, the unique face of evolution alive and awake, in you, as you, and through you. Some of our gifts are modest, private, and intimate; some are larger than life and have dramatic impact in the public sphere. Some of our gifts are actively given; others emerge from the very uniqueness of our being and presence.

Essence   This last point is subtle but essential. Unique Self contains in it
v.s   something of the old idea of "answering the call" that is essential
Blessing   in Kabbalah and Christian theology. But it is much more than that.
Your Unique Self expresses itself in your Unique Being as well as in
your Unique Becoming. Unique Self might have a public face, but
it can also be utterly private. A hermit may live Unique Self no less
than the president of the United States.

Station 6 C: Unique Vow, Unique Obligation

In the Buddhist tradition, the *bodhisattva* is one who seeks
Buddhahood through practicing noble action. The *bodhisattva*
vows to postpone his or her complete awakening and fulfillment
until all other beings are awakened and fulfilled. In Kabbalah this
same archetype is called the Tzadik. The determining factor in their
actions is compassion, deployed by utilizing the highest insight
and wisdom. The realization of Unique Self may be regarded as
bodhisattva activity, the unique manifestation of wisdom and
guidance. The Unique Self *bodhisattva* vow is an expression of
evolutionary joy and responsibility, even as it is a commitment to
the fulfillment of your evolutionary obligation.

Many of us recoil when we hear the word "obligation." We
identify obligation with arbitrarily imposed limitations set by the
church or state that suffocate the naturally free human being. Let's
inquire for a moment what obligation might mean at a higher level
of consciousness, rather than the obligation imposed by an authority
external to you. This inquiry yields the deeper truth that obligation
is the ultimate liberation. Obligation frees you from ambivalence
and allows you to commit 1,000 percent to the inherent invitation
that is the Unique Obligation present in every situation.

Obligation at this level of consciousness is created by the
direct and clear recognition of authentic need that can be uniquely
addressed by you and you alone. For example, let's say you are stuck
on a lush tropical island with another person. There is abundant
food. The problem is, due to a physical ailment, this person is
unable to feed herself. Are you obligated to feed her? Most people
would agree that in this situation, you have an absolute obligation

to feed her. Why is this so? It is based on what I call the fivefold principle of authentic obligation:

First, there is a need.
Second, it is a genuine and not a contrived need.
Third, you clearly recognize the need.
Fourth, you are capable of fulfilling the need.
Fifth, you realize that you are uniquely capable; the need can be uniquely addressed by you and you alone.

The combination of these five factors creates your Unique Obligation to give the Unique Gift that can be given only by you in this moment. Generally we cringe at the word obligation. We commonly understand obligation to be the opposite of love. In the original Hebrew, however, love and obligation are the same word. Authentic obligation is a natural by-product of authentic love.

Every true obligation is sourced in love. Unique love creates a Unique Obligation to give your Unique Gift. While most of our gifts address more subtle hungers than food, there is no person who does not possess Unique Gifts that respond to unique needs. From a non-dual perspective, it is your Unique Gift that creates your Unique Obligation. To live your Unique Self and offer your Unique Gift is to align yourself with the evolutionary impulse and fulfill your evolutionary obligation. *The realization of your Unique Self awakens you to the truth that there is a Unique Gift that your singular being and becoming offers the world, which is desperately needed by all-that-is and can be given by you and you alone.*

There is no more powerful and joyous realization available to a human being. It is the matrix of meaning that fills your life and is the core of your Unique Self enlightenment.

Before beginning the ten distinctions between Unique Self and Authentic Self, I simply note that although they are listed as distinct dimensions, they all overlap somewhat and are inextricably related. I speak of them as discrete distinctions as a way of pointing out the same essential discernment in its many different faces and implications.

CHAPTER 3:

DISTINCTIONS BETWEEN TWO MODELS OF THE SELF IN EVOLUTIONARY MYSTICISM

DISTINCTION ONE: THE AWAKENED PERSONAL AND IMPERSONAL FUNCTION

The following citation from Andrew Cohen's book *Evolutionary Enlightenment* sums up the critical chasm between the spiritual types that Unique Self and Authentic Self seek to foster. In the Authentic Self teaching, what is in the way of realizing enlightenment, or to borrow Roger Walsh's term, what is in the way of "spiritual maturity," is the following:

> "[M]ost of us have been brought up to believe that we are unique individuals, that we are special, that there is nobody quite like us" (p. 148).

The core distinction between the Unique Self teaching and the Authentic Self teaching lies in the very different vision each holds of the ideally enlightened spiritual self. The image that one holds of the awakened spiritual self is utterly essential as it creates the strange attractor towards which the entire spiritual system aspires. Particularly these two spiritual types have a radically different understanding of the relationship between the personal, the impersonal, and their place in spiritual life. Authentic Self, sometimes referred to as "Evolutionary Self," is taught as an "awakened impersonal function."[33] By contrast, Unique Self is radically personal. However, Unique Self is not the egoic personal self that we experience before we've awakened to the impersonal "no-self" state. Rather, Unique Self is the personal self which is characterized by "*irreducible* uniqueness" and is fully realized only after our awakening to the impersonal. The first level of personal, however—the separate self, ego, or personality—is also important to realization of Unique Self because the uniqueness at the level of ego after it is disambiguated by contact with the transcendent True Self points to the higher level personal of Unique Self. The Authentic Self model does not seem to draw this core distinction between these two forms of the personal, reducing all expressions of personal to what I have called level-one personal. The denial of any *ultimate* value to the personal comes from a conflation in the Authentic Self model of two strains of thought which each deny the personal from a different perspective. First, the denial comes from a particular strain of evolutionary spirituality, which sees the process as the only true reality and sees the personal as a lower level of consciousness that is to be overcome as one identifies with the larger evolutionary process. Second, the denial of the personal comes from the mystical schools of Advaita Vedanta and Theravada Buddhism, which view deconstructing the illusion of the personal and realizing True Self or No Self as the essence of enlightenment.

Further, *Evolutionary Enlightenment* says, "You are a process, dare to face this, and you will become transparent to yourself" (p.149).[34] The text also says, "Ultimately it reveals that the self

---

33   This is the description of Authentic Self as it appears in the audio series, *Awakening to Your Authentic Self* (2009, 2011). This term or some variant of it appears consistently throughout the Authentic Self teachings.

34   The text goes on to say, "I'm not denying that your experience *feels* personal.

is not a unique entity, but a process..." (p. 146). Or, later in the same chapter:

> "As you see through the illusion of the personal, you will recognize the truth that who we are as human beings is a bundle of impulses, reactions, and habits, conditioned patterns that together create the convincing appearance of unique individuality" (p. 149).

These citations seamlessly and probably unconsciously conflate the critique of the personal sourced in evolutionary metaphysics (the first two citations) and the old and tired Advaita Vedanata and Theravadan critique of self, (the third citation) which was already roundly rejected by Nagarjuna.[35]

Having said that, it is critical at the outset to state clearly once again that Unique Self is not a disguise for ego. The Unique Self teaching fully incorporates the True Self recognition of what the Buddhists call emptiness and what the Kabbalists call *Ayin*. On this, Unique Self and Authentic Self teaching agree. Unique Self realization is awakening to Uniqueness on the other side of emptiness, where the personal re-appears. In the Authentic Self teaching emergent from these early sources, the personal is repeatedly identified with two other words, separate and unique. That is, separate, unique, or personal is described as that which needs to be transcended in order to awaken into the realization of Authentic Self. The Unique Self teaching is built in part on making two clear distinctions between separateness and uniqueness, and between level-one personal, which is separate self, and level-two personal, which clarifies, after a realization of emptiness, as Unique Self. We will elaborate on this distinction between separateness and uniqueness briefly now as it is directly relevant to the limitation of

---

Your experience feels personal to you. My experience feels personal to me. The whole point, though, is that even that experience of it feeling personal is completely impersonal" (A. Cohen (2011), p. 149, emphasis in original).

35   For a brilliant analysis of Nagurjuna's critique of the Therevadan postion of no self, see Ken Wilber, *Sex Ecology and Spirituality* (1995), ch.14, fn. 1, pp. 717.

the personal to what I have termed level-one personal, the personal before the impersonal, and then return to this discernment for further elaboration in distinction three below.[36]

In realizing that the separate self is an illusion[37] which is the source of most suffering,[38] a number of schools of mysticism, including many expressions of Advaita Vedanta, Theravada Buddhism, and certain strains in early Hassidism, made a significant mistake: they confused separateness and uniqueness. The axiomatic assumption in many of these classical enlightenment teachings—in both their ancient and modern expressions—is that to transcend the separate self, you must leave behind not only the illusion of separation, but also the apparent experience of uniqueness. Much effort in classical True Self enlightenment teaching was directed into demonstrating that what seemed to be unique and particular was, in fact, common and universal, and what seemed to be personal was actually impersonal. There was great truth in some of this teaching, and it clearly brought immense spiritual depth and some measure of peace to many. And yet, the core teaching did not take root among the masses. The problem

36   This distinction allows for a full integration of Western and Eastern models of enlightenment in the higher integral embrace of Unique Self. The core contradiction lies between the dominant motifs and moods of Eastern and Western spirituality. Eastern and Western spirituality each make a critical mistake based on an essential confusion between separateness and uniqueness. Each made the same mistake, in the opposite manner.

37   A more accurate statement about ego identity or separate self identity would not label it an illusion of identity, but rather point out that it is a limited identity. Separate self is real in the mind of God and the mind of men. Ego identity is part of the human identity, but it is a limited part of human identity. Human identity is not exhausted by ego identity. Human identity transcends and includes ego identity. This kind of re-wording is essential in contemporary enlightenment teaching.

38   Classical mysticism, by and large, rightly sees the separate self as an illusion. The realization of this illusion comes from profound spiritual practices, like meditation, which work to open the eye of the spirit. Not only is the separate self exposed as an illusion, it is also the root source of most human suffering. Fear, death, terror, and cruelty in virtually all of their forms can ultimately be traced back to the illusion of the separate self. It is for this most compelling of reasons that mystical schools devoted an enormous amount of energy to dispelling the illusion of the separate ego self.

was not simply that the masses were lazy, stupid, or in lower states of consciousness, as some teachers asserted. The deeper problem was that the masses felt that the teaching violated their basic sense of the necessity, desirability, and dignity of uniqueness.

The problem was—and is—that uniqueness will just not go away. The majority of people correctly feel that to surrender their uniqueness would be to surrender their life force, as well as their personal value and dignity. The personal is, by it's very nature, *unique*. The dignity and value of the personal derives directly from its uniqueness. The most powerful and authentic experience of one's own uniqueness appears, paradoxically, after and not before the dissolution of ego. Many mystical teachings in these schools try valiantly to explain this away by telling the student in many different ways that their lingering experience of personal uniqueness is merely evidence that they have not yet evolved beyond ego. But the student intuits that this is simply not true. Uniqueness is experienced not merely as an expression of ego, but as a glorious expression of one's truest nature. The student understands that she is part of the seamless coat of the Uni-verse, which is indeed seamless, but not featureless. In the realization of Unique Self, she understands that her personal uniqueness is the highest expression of God looking out from behind her eyes. Hence, to awaken, the student must move beyond separate self, even as she must embrace and affirm her unique—personal— individuation beyond ego. Because these schools demand that the student throw out personal uniqueness as part of dispelling the illusion of the ego or the separate self, the student correctly rebels against this dharma. The student intuitively affirms the value of the personal. Impersonality feels like a violation of the very quality of divine humanness that she holds most dear.[39] The West has essentially ignored the call to evolve beyond separate-self ego, and most of humanity has remained stuck with the ego and all of its attendant horrors.

In classical spiritual thought God is thought of as the infinity of power. In some strains of thought that power is externalized to

---

39 See the chart in Appendix B for more on the stations of Unique Self.

the cosmos, classic exoteric theism. In other strains, that power is interior to the cosmos, classic exoteric pantheism. In more esoteric versions of both theism and pantheism, this distinction is effaced as immanence and transcendence are held in paradoxical complimentarity. In the awakened realization of Unique Self, however, God is not merely the infinity of power—in whatever way that story is told—but the infinity of intimacy, both the intimacy that limns the cosmos and the intimacy that knows your name and holds you in every moment. You, human being reading this page, you are not absorbed by but rather affirmed by that intimacy. Said simply, you are God's Unique Intimacy. That is the essence of Unique Self awakening.

By contrast, in the Authentic Self teaching, one awakens to the impersonal face of the process, expressing itself in you and as you. This is the creative evolutionary impulse that moves through you. In Unique Self, or what I have called Evolutionary Unique Self, you awaken to the irreducibly personal face of the process, the creative evolutionary God impulse living in you, as you, and through you. The difference is far from semantic. It has profound implications in virtually every dimension of life, from ethics to psychology, spirituality, sexuality, economics, relationships, death and dying, parenting, and just about everything else.

DISTINCTION TWO: UNIQUE VALUE
AND IMPERSONAL PROCESS[40]

The following four claims represent accurately some of the core motifs of the Authentic Self model:

> "From the radically impersonal point of view of the evolution of consciousness, your **ultimate value** lies in your potential to awaken to the evolutionary impulse as

---

40 It's important to note here that this is not the "process" of Process philosophy or theology, but rather is specific to these teachings. Also, on the important topic of "dialectical materialism" and the devastating effects of the impersonal process, see Steve McIntosh (2012). See also the endnote discussing models of evolution in relationship to spirituality.

your own Authentic Self... *That's* what the process wants. That's why we are each so desperately needed" (p. 122, first emphasis added, second emphasis in original).

"God, as the creative impulse, or Eros, is interested in you for your higher potentials, for what you are *capable* of; **God isn't interested in you as a personal self**" (p. 122, first emphasis in original, second emphasis added).

"You are a potential bearer of the future, and therefore the impulse that is driving the evolutionary process is **only** interested in you according to how much of that potential you are able to fulfill" (p. 122, emphasis added).

"The drama of your personal concerns and desires is, if not irrelevant, **always secondary** to the prime directive of the authentic self, which is the evolution of the process itself" (p. 153, emphasis added).

This set of four passages is troubling. History has shown the catastrophes that have resulted from philosophies in which the individual, the personal, is always secondary to and subsumed under the greater good of the process or the march of history.[4]

When a tradition or teaching fails to hold the infinite, absolute, and irreducible dignity of the personal, then even if all the teachers in the system are personal saints, the structures of teachings themselves allow for future devolution into a system that supports all forms of unethical wielding of authority, which are in violation of the fundamental, infinite, personal dignity of every individual. We, who see ourselves at the "leading edge," laying down new dharma tracks within an Integral framework, must take responsibility not only for ourselves, but also for the implications, even if unintended, of our teaching over the generations. Authority structures which began to see themselves as aligned with or even identical with the "process," placing the personal as secondary, which was the teaching of Hegel, tragically gave birth to some of the darkest teachings of Social Darwinism and later the manifest evils of Fascism, Communism, and Nazism.

This statement, of course, is not to suggest that the teachers of Authentic Self have any connection to or responsibility for these distortions of evolutionary spirituality from history, much in the same way that we wouldn't hold contemporary Christian thinkers responsible for the old structures in Christian thought which contributed to the holocaust or myself for the distortion of biblical thinking that produced extreme expressions of abominable racist politics. What we are all responsible for is the development of foundational frameworks that we lay down now as source code thinkers. We need to be wary of potential distortions of these and their moral implications. We need to shine light on the dark shadow of forms of evolutionary spirituality which insists on the primacy of the process over the individual. In the same way that we correctly challenge the great traditions of the religions whose theological frameworks allow for the evils of religious wars and exploitation, even when that was not the initial intention of the religion, so too we must call evolutionary spirituality to account for the evils committed in its name or under the influence of its spirit.[41] More important, however, we must correct the foundational imbalances at the very core of certain expressions of evolutionary spirituality in order to insure to the best of our ability that it is a healing and not destructive dharma as it works the source code of both culture and the interiors of the individual student.

Most of the aforementioned expressions of evil were profoundly influenced by Hegel's teaching that demanded that the individual awaken and identify with the great evolutionary process of divine unfolding in Absolute Spirit. In Hegel's powerful clarion call to align with the ecstatic impulse of historically unfolding evolutionary God, the holiness of the individual was somehow crushed in all the grand rhetoric, with devastating results for God and humans. This is but one of the reasons that the Unique Self teaching is partially sourced in the ethical matrix of what I have

---

41   See the notes section at the end of this book for a discussion by A. Combs and S. Krippner (1996) on three distinct notions of evolution in relationship to spirituality.

termed Evolutionary Kabbalah.[42] Of the essence of Evolutionary Kabbalah, not only but especially in its non-dual expressions, is that *the process must always remain personal.* For me, it was always the Hasidic master Levi Isaac of Berdichev who radically reminded me of the primacy of the personal even when in the throes of evolutionary ecstasy. Levi Isaac was once leading the prayers at the close of Yom Kippur services. Yom Kippur is a fast day and the holiest day in the Hebrew calendar. The twilight hours at the end of the fast are filled with potency.

According to the evolutionary mystics of Kabbalah, the enlightened prayer leader, during that time, may potentially enter the virtual source code of reality and affect a *tikkun;* that is, affect a momentous leap in the evolution of consciousness for the sake of all sentient beings, in all generations. This is precisely what Levi Isaac—greatest of all enlightened evolutionary prayer leaders—was doing on that Yom Kippur. Night had already fallen, the fast was officially over, but the ecstasy of Levi Isaac was rippling through all the upper worlds. All beings held their breath in awe of the evolutionary power of Levi Isaac's consciousness. All of reality was pulsating with him towards an ecstatic evolutionary crescendo. And just as the great breakthrough was about to happen at the leading edge, Levi Isaac spotted, out of the corner of his eye, an old man who was thirsty. The fast had been very long, and the old man needed to drink. And so, in the midst of his ecstasy, Levi Isaac brought the whole evolutionary process to a halt. He immediately ended the fast and personally brought the old man a drink of water.[43] This is very different from a teaching which insists time and again that "The drama of your personal concerns and desires is, if not irrelevant, **always secondary** to the prime directive of the authentic self, which is the evolution of the process itself" (p. 153, emphasis added). Levi Isaac in this story

---

42   Back in 2004 I promised Ken Wilber a book on Integral Kabbalah. I hope that this book will fulfill that promise. For some of the primary teachings of Evolutionary Kabbalah, see marcgafni.com under the tab "Evolutionary Kabbalah."

43   On this story, see L. Jacobs (1992).

is actively engaged in "creating the future." The future in all of its gravitas and glory, however, is always secondary to the infinite dignity of the personal—in this case, an old man who needed a glass of water.

There is, however, a second, kabbalistic-evolutiouary reading of the story that points to another apparently false dichotomy in the Authentic Self teaching. From the perspective of Levi Isaac, bringing the man a glass of water had evolutionary implications. The split in the citations above between engagement in the personal and the evolutionary is fallacious. Unique Self teachings demand that you see your entire life—everything that you live, breathe, feel, think, or desire on all levels of your Being—within the larger framework of your direct participation in the evolution of God. It is this larger context that is the key to your liberation. The proto Unique Self mystics of the Kabbalah have taught for generations that every human action should be preceded by an affirmative statement of meaning: "I do this act for the sake of unifying and evolving divinity."[44] When every significant action you take is for the sake of the all, infused with a profound awareness of your evolutionary context, you stop reacting from ego and begin acting from the place of a powerful evolutionary integrity. Renaissance kabbalist Isaac Luria developed a highly elaborate series of evolutionary *kavvanot,* intentions. Each was a formal affirmation said at a different moment during the day, in order to awaken and align the intention of the individual with the evolutionary divine context in which they lived and breathed.

For Isaac Luria, arguably the most significant kabbalist of the last five hundred years, the ecstatic human obligation to awaken to Unique Self is the primary source of joy. It is the giving of your Unique Gift that fills your life with direction, meaning,

---

44 See here L. Fine (1986, 1987) in his articles "The Art of Metoposcopy: A Study in Isaac Luria's Charismatic Knowledge" and "The Contemplative Practice of Yichudim." The phrase is my free translumination of the original hebrew/aramaic formula, *"Leshem Yichud Kudsha Berik Hu, Ushechentei," "for the sake of the unification of the divine masculine and divine feminine."* The word *Yichud,* unification, is often synonymous in Hebrew mystical texts with *Tikkun. Tikkun* means to heal, repair, or evolve.

and delight. The split between the personal and the impersonal disappears as you awaken to your unique *tikkun* (fixing) in the larger context of the field of all life that ever was, is, and will be. It is for this reason that there is little talk in the Kabbalah about individual enlightenment. The danger of excessive emphasis on the individual is that you become a spiritual narcissist, totally focused on your experience of freedom and spaciousness. You then confuse that with Liberation, which it is not. *Enlightenment is an embodied activist relation to reality infused with evolutionary integrity, which is far beyond the awakening of True Self.* To be fully awake is to incarnate both the ethical impulse of the personal and the utopian impulse of the impersonal. Any spiritual path that undermines the infinite adequacy and dignity of the personal, in the end, undermines all that is good, true, and beautiful. The infinite personal dignity and value of each and every Unique Self is the noble matrix of interpersonal ethics and obligation. It must, therefore, be affirmed with undying passion.

At the same time to confuse level-one personal with level-two personal—separate self and Unique Self—is to reduce the personal to the mere grasping ego. For example, to not awaken to the impersonal, expressed as a profound consciousness of the larger evolutionary context, would undermine the evolutionary ethos that moves us to act for the sake of the all. And then, beyond the impersonal, the higher personal comes back online with the deeper realization that the process is ultimately personal at its core.

In the kabbalistic teaching, everything takes place in the larger evolutionary context of community and for the sake of the larger whole. And yet, the whole is never quite reduced to a process. Somehow in both the liberation teaching and the lived communities of the kabbalists, the sacred and paradoxical tension between the individual and the process was held in fine attunement. This is very different from the teaching of Authentic Self which sharply distinguishes between the personal and the evolutionary, placing the personal at odds "with the expanded and deepened" absolute context of your life.

Another passage in *Evolutionary Enlightenment* asks:

"Does this mean you will cease to care about your personal relationships, your connection to your ethnic roots, or the culture from which you have come? No. But it *does* mean that something else has become *more important* to you because the context for the life you are living has dramatically expanded and deepened" (p. 153, emphasis in original).

While this passage and three or four others assign what the Authentic Self teachings call, in a different passage, "relative" value to the realm of the personal, it is clear that it is regarded as without primary importance. What is most important, clearly more important than the intrinsic value of the individual, is the impersonal process, which is in passage after passage equated with the evolutionary impulse and deified explicitly as the totality of God.[45] The individual is always secondary to the process:

"In that [evolutionary] impulse, there is no other motive than to create the future, unceasingly, and the needs of any individual are **always secondary** to that greater purpose" (p. 157 emphasis added).

DISTINCTION THREE:
EVOLUTIONARY LOVE VS. ABSOLUTE LOVE

From this process perspective that *Evolutionary Enlightenment* lays out, evidenced for example in the quote we just saw in the preceding paragraph, love itself becomes fundamentally impersonal. This set of equations are implicitly laid out time and again: God = evolutionary impulse = love. But: "[I]t is an impersonal, wild,

---

45 The evolutionary impulse is a third person process. It is an expression of the impersonal third person face of God. There is, however, both a first person face of God in which God appears in you as you in the most personal and intimate sense, as well as a second person face of God in which god appears as the personal quality of the infinity of intimacy that holds you, sustains you, supports you, and knows you in every moment. To identify God only with the third person face is an egregious limitation, a defacing of divinity.

fierce, unyielding love that cares **only** about the evolution of the process, and not necessarily about the personal circumstance of any particular individual" (p. 91, emphasis added). Other Authentic Self teachings identify personal love as not worthy of being even called by the same name as absolute love. As Andrew said in that dialogue, if absolute impersonal experience of relation is called love, then the relative personal expression of relation cannot be called love. They cannot fairly be called by the same name.

In the Unique Self teaching, there is a continuum of love in which both personal and absolute love participate in the same essential quality.[46]

This distinction requires further elaboration. The Authentic Self teaching emergent from classical Buddhism and Advaita Vedanta makes a strong distinction between the absolute and relative realm of reality. There is a sharp distinction drawn between the "impersonal" and the "evolution of consciousness," which is the realm of the absolute and "your so-called personal life" (p. 154), which is the realm of the merely "relative." "Your personal sphere, your intimate and historical relationships, your unique personality" (p. 60) are "relative," while the impersonal Authentic Self, which is the "impersonal evolutionary impulse," is "absolute." Love that is not "interested in you personally" is "absolute love."

In 2010, I did two dialogues with Andrew Cohen in the Future of Love series, one on Unique Self and Authentic Self, and the second on love. Not long afterwards, Andrew published a blog post on love, entitled "'I Just Called to Say I Love You': Reflections on the Multiple Meanings of Love." (The reference citation is an updated version of the earlier blog post.) The dharmic assumptions in the blog posts were troubling to me. I wrote Andrew in that regard, and we agreed to do a recorded dialogue on the topic. Andrew offered a compelling and articulate restatement of the core position in his blog post. He said both in the post and in the dialogue that the difference between relative love, which was personal, and absolute love, which was impersonal, was so immense that in reality they could not even be called by the same name:

---

46 See Gafni (2012), "Evolutionary Love."

"Having the direct experience of the absolute nature of spiritual love, or, to put it in theological language, the love of God, changes our understanding of what love is and what it means, forever. Now we can no longer mistake that which is merely personal and relative for that which is always impersonal and absolute. Once again, this is a significant distinction that a lot of spiritually minded people miss: the all-important difference between spiritual love, which is absolute, and non-spiritual or personal love, which is relative...they cannot be called by the same name"

In response, I argued that from an evolutionary perspective, there was really no distinction at all between relative and absolute love. The same love that initiated the big bang, is the evolutionary eros that animates all of reality. It is the same love that causes quarks to come together to form atoms. Eros or love by any other name is the movement towards higher and higher levels of mutuality, recognition, union, and embrace. It moves atoms to become molecules, and then later, complex molecules. It moves cell to become multicelluar beings. Love, the movement towards higher and higher levels of mutuality, recognition, union, and embrace is the eros driving all of evolution. It is the force of allurement, the omega point or strange attractor that pulls all of reality to higher and deeper levels of complexity and consciousness.

Eventually, the evolutionary chain reaches the triune brain. Cultural evolution is born, which takes man through many structure stages of consciousness, each one demarcated by higher levels of mutuality, recognition, union, and embrace. The human being herself then moves to higher and higher levels of consciousness. All of this is the evolution of love. The human being begins with ego-centric love, which is a felt sense of care and concern for her immediate circle of intimates. She then evolves to ethnocentric love, which is a felt sense of care and concern for the entire tribe. Then, she evolves to world-centric love, a felt sense of care and concern for every human being on the planet. It is at the world-centric level that a clear sense of Unique Self begins to show up.

Finally, she evolves to kosmo-centric, where her felt sense of caring and concern is for all sentient and non-sentient beings.

She realizes her full divinity and shifts her perspective from "her side" to "God's side" and loves with the divine love that initiated the cosmos. From this perspective, one understands that all love is part of a continuum, and all love is sourced in the same evolutionary love that initiated all-that-is. Absolute- and relative-love are, at source, One Love. This is relevant to our issues because it demonstrates the fallacy of this position in radically splitting between the relative and absolute forms of love. And, of course, relative love is precisely what we might call personal love. In effect, this is another example of the systemic devaluation of the personal relative to the impersonal that is the hallmark of the Authentic Self teaching. In the Unique Self teaching, the personal itself is an expression of the absolute. The split between the absolute and the relative is effaced from the non-dual awakened perspective of Unique Self because, in the final analysis, emptiness is form and form is emptiness. All form is therefore Unique. In the course of evolution, there is movement to higher and higher levels of complexity, consciousness, and uniqueness. In effect, the trajectory of evolution is in some core sense about the evolution of eros, creativity, and uniqueness, which are different faces of the same one.

The evolution of eros and love—the movement towards higher levels of mutuality, recognition, union, and embrace—creates higher and higher levels of creativity. Creativity is a function of unique perspective and insight. And the virtuous circle of evolution continues. As uniqueness evolves, it awakens. The same is true as we saw above for evolution itself. Evolution moves from unconscious to conscious evolution. Uniqueness moves along the trajectory of evolution from unconscious to conscious uniqueness. The more conscious uniqueness becomes, the more personal it becomes. An atom may be unique, but it has only a modicum of personal quality. A human being is more personal the more he/she is awake, aware of his/her particular uniqueness, and able to make contact with the uniqueness of an Other.

In this sense, from a Unique Self perspective, the evolution of uniqueness is the evolution of intimacy. In the realization of Unique Self, the inner essence of reality is the infinity of intimacy. This is the realization that, at its core, consciousness is love—the evolution of consciousness is, therefore, nothing less than the evolution of love. If you then realize that God is synonymous with love, you begin to understand that the evolution of love is no less than the evolution of God. God is the infinite. The infinite is the intimate. God is the infinity of intimacy. This intimacy comes into fullness with the awakening of the Evolutionary Unique Self, which is the full human awakening to God in first, second, and third persons. The human being is called by God to be God and to incarnate the evolutionary love that initiated and animates all-that-is.

Awakening as the Love Intelligence of the Evolutionary Unique Self

It is not enough to awaken only to your Unique Expression of True Self. There is a second critical dimension of awakening that is essential to Unique Self realization. I received a direct transmission of this second dimension of Unique Self enlightenment from my lineage teachers who are best described as evolutionary mystics.

Isaac Luria, the teacher of my teachers, the great evolutionary mystic of the Renaissance period, taught that every action that a person takes must be with the explicit consciousness and intention of *tikkun*. *Tikkun* is best translated as the evolutionary healing and transformation of all of reality. Every action must be invested with evolutionary intention. In Luria's language, it must be *leshem yichud*, meaning for the sake of the evolutionary integration and transformation of all of reality. The core intention that informs the evolutionary process is for Luria no less then eros or love itself. This core Lurianic teaching is unpacked at great length and depth in post-Lurianic thought from Luria's close student Hayyim Vital to Moshe Chaim Luzatto all the way through early and later forms of hassidism. Stated clearly, for Luria, the expression and evolution of love is the essential purpose, driving force, and animating eros of an evolutionary reality.

In the language of the Hebrew evolutionary mystics themselves, to awaken to your Unique Self is to "shift your perspective." The way the evolutionary mystics say it is simply to shift your perspective from "your side" to "God's side." To shift your perspective is to become a lover—for to be a lover is no more and no less then to see the face of other with God's eyes. To see with God's eyes, the eye of the heart, is an essential definition of enlightenment for the Hebrew evolutionary mystics of Unique Self. It is the core of a practice which is central to my life and my inner circle of students which we call "loving your way to enlightenment." To the evolutionary mystics, to awaken means not necessarily to have a profound mystical state experience in which you feel all of Being living in you; rather, to awaken is to dramatically, yet simply, shift your alignment. To no longer align with your will, but with God's will. But not only. It is to awaken to love. Not with your limited love, but with the love intelligence that is the intiating and animating eros of all-that-is, awake and alive in you. Your personal love is an expression of the personal quality of divinity. To see with the eyes of love is to make the evolutionary eros conscious, to see with God's eyes. And the essence of love as it is expressed inter-subjectively is no less than Unique Self perception. A word of elaboration is in order here on the nature of intersubjective love as a Unique Self perception as this understanding is one of the core distinctions between the Unique Self and Authentic Self models of love. In the section below, I will somewhat depart from the more third person tone of this article, which was written as an academic paper for the Integral Theory Conference in 2013. I will, with your indulgence, dear reader, move from a more third-person form of analysis to a more integrated, first-, second-, and third person form of writing.

On the Nature of Inter-Subjective Love

It was September 11, 2001. The planes had just crashed into the Twin Towers in Manhattan. People had very short moments to use their cell phones. No one called asking for revenge. No one offered philosophical explanations or profound insights into the nature of reality. People did one thing and one thing only: they called the people close to their heart to say, "I love you." "I love you" is our declaration of faith. Implicit in those words is everything holy.

And yet we no longer really know what we mean when we say, "I love you." It used to mean, "I am committed to you. I will live with you forever." Or it might have meant, "You are the most important person in my life." But it no longer seems to mean that. The old Greek, Thucydides, wrote in his great work *The Peloponnesian War* something like, "When words lose their meaning, culture collapses." When you no longer understand your own deepest declarations of love, you are lost. The very foundation of meaning upon which your world rests is undermined. You lose your way. You become alienated from love, which is your home. Despair, addiction, and numbness become your constant companions.

For so many of us, love has lost its luminosity as the organizing principle of our lives. Love seems to have diminished power to locate us and to guide us home. "I love you" has become banal, casual, and desiccated.

One day you feel the love; the next day you do not. One day love holds you in the place of your belonging, and the very next day you are cast out, exiled, and lost. For so many of us, "I love you" has ceased to be a place where we can find our home.

What do you really mean when your highest self says to another, "I love you"?

And if I might audaciously add to the question: why do all the great traditions, in one way or another, talk about the obligation to love God and love your neighbor? In the tradition of Kabbalah, this obligation to love God and one another is called a *mitzvah temidit*, a "constant obligation of consciousness." But does this truly resonate with our experience? Actually, if we admit it to ourselves, this injunction makes little sense. How does a human being love God? Is God lovable? Can you touch God, cuddle with God, or actually feel rushing love for God without entering into an altered state?

What emotional affect is there to the love of God? And does not that emotional affect, if it is even an authentic possibility for the common person, seem dangerously close to a kind of blind fundamentalist emotional faith?

How does one love God? And how can one be obligated to love another? How can you obligate an emotion? And can we truly feel love toward all of our neighbors? Isn't love reserved for the very few special people in our lives?

Said differently and more directly, what is love?

To know the way of Unique Self, you must know the way of love.

To find your destination in love, you must consider the reason for all of your detours. You must wonder about all of your wrong turns in love.

Where did you go wrong? Is there something you did not understand about the nature of love?

You are not alone in your questions. There is hardly a person alive who is conscious who has not asked these questions—this writer included. So I will speak to myself through you.

Love is a Verb

If you are like most highly intelligent and sincere modern seekers, you are making two core mistakes about love. First, you think that love is, at its core, both an emotion and a noun.

When the emotion is gone, you feel like you are no longer in love and thus can no longer stay in the relationship.

Second, you automatically identify love with a particular emotion. The emotion with which you identify love is usually the emotion of infatuation. Both of these mistaken beliefs are significant obstacles on your path to spiritual liberation. Both of these mistakes obscure love's innate ability to take you home.

Love at its core is not an emotion or a noun. Love is a perception. Love is the ultimate verb. Love is a faculty of perception that allows you to see the inner nature of All-That-Is.

To love another human being is to perceive their True Nature. To love is to perceive the infinite specialness and divine beauty of the beloved.

To be a lover is to see beyond the limited and distorting vision of your separate-self contraction.

To be a lover is to see with God's eyes. Your beloved is both your lover and All-That-Is.

To love another human being is to perceive their True Nature. To love is to perceive the infinite specialness and divine beauty of the beloved.

To be a lover is to see beyond the limited and distorting vision of your separate-self contraction.

To be a lover is to see with God's eyes. Your beloved is both your lover and All-That-Is.

To be loved by another human being is to have your True Nature seen. Your True Nature is your Unique Self.

To love God is to let God see with your eyes, to empower God with the vision of your Unique Perspective. You are living out of a passion for God. You are being asked to live with God's eyes.

To act with God's eyes, to react with God's eyes, to write your Book of Life with God's eyes as God would see from your perspective. If you are successful, then your perspective becomes available to God. It finds God and feeds God. It gives God strength and joy. *You must consider that being a devotee is nothing but actually being God from a distinct perspective.*

This is the only truth about individuality. Mature individuality is not about being separate. It is about having a distinct perspective within the context of Union.

To be responsible for this perspective is to declare the truth from this vantage point, but without making it the only perspective, and without any degree of attachment to the vantage point we have clung to from the past—from our previous conditioning. This is what it means to be a lover.

This is the great paradox again and again. *To be a lover is to see with God's eyes. To love God is to let God see with your eyes.*

Love is a Unique Self Perception

Once, I shared this understanding of love with the Dalai Lama. "Beautiful!" he exclaimed with sheer and utter delight.

Beautiful was the Dalai Lama in the direct and delicious expression of his delight. Particularly, he was excited to shift the understanding of love from an emotion to a perception.

It is this precise shift that clears up one of the great mysteries of love. Many great thinkers have been puzzled by the Hebrew wisdom commandment to love. How can you command an emotion? And yet in the evolutionary mysticism of Unique Self teaching, love is the ultimate commandment. Reading the old Hebrew text, "Love your neighbor as yourself—I AM GOD," the answer to the puzzle is now clear.

Step one: Love is not, at its core, an emotion or a noun. Love is a perception.

"Love your neighbor as yourself" is the seemingly impossible demand of the Hebrew book of Leviticus, echoed in the New Testament in the book of Matthew. At least this is how the text is usually cited. But the quote, as it is usually cited, is actually missing three words. It's too short. What all too often gets left out of the passage are the three last, and perhaps most crucial, words. The complete verse is, "Love your neighbor as yourself—I AM GOD." To love your neighbor is to know that the "I" is God. *To love your neighbor is to perceive God's divine beauty in others and let it fill you with wonder and radical amazement.* To love your neighbor is to behold with wonder God's infinite specialness. Love is what the Hindus called *bhakti,* to truly see the other bathed in their own divine radiance.

Love is not merely an emotion or a noun. Love is not but infatuation.

Emotions are involuntary reactions that come from the nervous system. The emotion of infatuation is usually a preprogrammed reaction that takes place when you meet someone that you recognize. You recognize them because you remember them. They evoke in you a sense of familiarity and intimacy. They unconsciously remind you of your parents or early caretakers.

The person with whom you are infatuated holds out to you the possibility of completing the unfinished emotional business you have with your mother, father, or early caretakers. Or you fall in love with them as an expression of your unconscious rebellion or alienation from your parents or caretakers, whom you experience as painful or dangerous. The people who have best recapitulated and evolved the classic literature on this dynamic are my dear friends and colleagues Harville and Helen Hendrix in their important work called Imago therapy. Love, however, as both Harville and Helen recognize, is much more then this level of unconscious attraction. Love is a divine eros, and when it awakens, it is a genuine form of divine seeing.

Only when you fall out of infatuation do you see—sometimes for the first time. Before then, your perception is blurred. Infatuation is blind. Love is a magnifying glass. Initially the perception yields a more complex and less rosy picture than the blind adulation of infatuation, but if you stay with it, remain focused, and invest yourself with full passion and heart, the perception begins to clarify. You begin to genuinely see the full splendor and beauty of the one you love. The delight of love is a natural result of your perceptions. This is, however, not the full extent of love. It is not divorced from the absolute love that is the animating eros of all-that-is. Rather, conscious personal love is the awakened form of evolutionary love. Much like evolution moves from unconscious to conscious evolution, and uniqueness evolves from unconscious to conscious uniqueness, eros and love evolve from unconscious eros and love to conscious eros and love. The impersonal reveals its true essence as the personal.

Love is perception's gift. Love is a faculty of perception, which allows you to see the inner nature of All-That-Is. Love is a realization. *Love is a verb. Love is the true inner nature of All-That-Is. Love is.*

To very briefly recapitulate then, to be an awakened lover is to see with God's eyes. To love God is to let God see through your eyes.

We do not mean God here in the old mythic sense of the ethnocentric God who created the world in six days and is anti-science, vengeful, and anti-humanity. By God, Luria refers to the evolutionary process of unfolding which drives and animates the kosmos on every level of existence. God's will is the will of the kosmos. God is what Aurobindo refers to in his great work *The Future Evolution of Man* as the "evolutionary imperative," or what has been more recently renamed as the "Evolutionary Impulse" (Hubbard, 1998). It is the creative force of the kosmos, which is, intends, and moves all-that-is toward healing and transformation. It is the evolutionary impulse that lives in you, as you, and through you. And God is also infinitely personal—the infinity of intimacy that holds you in your pain and delights in your joy and knows your name. We will return to the personal face of the divine as it emerges from Unique Self teaching in Distinction Seven: "Authentic Self, Unique Self, and the Personal Face of God," below.

To awaken to your Unique Self means to awaken to the impulse to evolve, which is the divine creativity surging in you at this very moment, reaching toward the good, the true, and the beautiful. Evolution is spirit in action. The great Einsteins of consciousness in all great traditions understood that the interior of spirit or consciousness is love. Evolution there is not less than love in action.

To awaken to your Unique Self is to realize—as the evolutionary mystics taught us—that you live in an evolutionary context. Love is not merely a quality of being; it is also the Eros of becoming. To awaken to your Unique Self is to realize that your True Self is neither without unique quality, without level,[47] nor is it static. When we thought that the divine field was an eternal absolute, then naturally we felt that the realization of True Self was the awakening to your unqualified eternal, absolute, and unchanging consciousness. Love as Being. The evolutionary mystics, however, from Luria to Schelling to Kook to Aurobindo, awakened to the evolving nature of spirit. *Evolution is love in action.*

As we moved into modernity and Darwinian science, the contemporary evolutionary mystics realized that their initial insight into the evolution of spirit applied not only to spirit, but also to the evolution of the biosphere, of the physical world. My teacher Abraham Kook, as cited above,[48] writes, "all of reality"— matter, body, mind, soul, and spirit—"is always evolving." To be a mystic is to know something of the interior face of the kosmos, which is love. The novice today who had received the accumulated knowing of the past knows today what only the most advanced

---

47 True Self is always refracted through your particular level or structure stage of consciousness—for example, egocentric, ethnocentric, worldcentric, or kosmoscentric.

48 Kook, A.Y. n.d. Teaching on evolution. *Lights of holiness.* (M. Gafni, Trans.).

souls knew five hundred years ago, that evolutionary love is the inner mechanism of mystery.

For example, Renaissance mystic Isaac Luria and his school of Kabbalists had a deep knowing of the inner evolutionary process of spirit. They knew through deep mystical contemplation that the awakened human being was actively and consciously engaging as irreducible expressions of love intelligence in the evolution of all of reality. In their more audacious non-dual formulations, these evolutionary mystics, writing in the 16th century, realized that man is responsible for the evolution of God.

They understood and clearly articulated that the specific privilege and wild responsibility of the human being is to awaken to conscious evolution, which is identical with conscious love. And, these very evolutionary mystics are the original inspiration for the core teaching of Unique Self. This is substantively different from the Authentic Self teachings. For Authentic Self, enlightenment, in Andrew Cohen's teaching, is an "awakened impersonal function." By contrast, Unique Self is the personal after the impersonal and is characterized by irreducible uniqueness.

True love is impersonal or absolute love. In the non-dual realization of Unique Self, the entire distinction between the absolute and the relative is in part effaced. The ego prefigures the Unique Self. True Self clarifies the distortions of the relative to allow the Unique Self to emerge as the unique expression of absolute love.

Unique Self is the personal after the impersonal and is characterized by irreducible uniqueness. Love is personal at its core. Personal love and impersonal love exist on the same continuum and participate in the same essential quality. Rather than saying, as the Authentic Self teaching does, that these two cannot even share the same name, Unique Self teaching affirms that not only do they share the same name and essence, but and this is key, awakened conscious personal love is the highest evolutionary expression of love. Personal love is more evolved than impersonal love. The impersonal love that moves the sun and the stars awaken from unconscious to conscious love in the personal love, commitment, and loyalty that exists in freely chosen form between human beings.

In this broader evolutionary mystical context, it is possible to say simply that in the awakened Unique Self, evolution becomes conscious of itself. It is the awakened Unique Self feeling the imperative of evolution consciously alive in herself that is therefore called to give her Unique Gifts for the sake of the evolution of all of reality. So, the Unique Self in full realization might be more accurately termed the evolutionary Unique Self. The awakened Unique Self who has evolved beyond exclusive identification with ego is constantly being called by the evolutionary impulse. Indeed, it is in consciously aligning his Unique Self will with the evolutionary will of the kosmos that the human being is pulled beyond ego to True Self, and then to the personal face of True Self—Unique Self. One does not escape ego by awakening to the evolutionary Unique Self. Ego is always present. However, by identifying with the infinitely larger context of the evolutionary Unique Self, the limited identification with ego is gloriously trance-ended. (For a graphic representation of these stations of consciousness, see the chart in Appendix B.)

DISTINCTION FOUR:
THE PERSONAL IS REALLY IMPERSONAL VS. THE IMPERSONAL IS ALSO PERSONAL

For Authentic Self, the realm of the personal is in the most positive passages in *Evolutionary Spirituality*, an "outer sheath" and "secondary." True reality for Authentic Self is found in the realm of the impersonal. The personal is viewed by Authentic Self as an illusion. In fact, a fourth distinction between Authentic Self and Unique Self is that, for Authentic Self, the personal itself is really impersonal. The personal is such an anathema to the Authentic Self teaching that, in the teaching, there is a striking attempt not only to invalidate the personal, or locate the personal only at what I have termed level-one personal, (the level of ego or separate self), but also to reduce the personal to the impersonal. In the following four citations, that is precisely the argument being made. The process produced everything, these passages argue, and since the process is impersonal, the impersonal created the personal. That means in the Authentic Self teaching that the personal simply does not exist. This is, of course, the result of conflating the primacy of the process prevalent in the dialectical materialism of Hegelian and later Marxist evolutionary spirituality and the view of Advaita Vedanta and later Theravada Buddhism that the personal is an illusion to be overcome at virtually all costs. This conflation, as noted earlier, deals a deathblow to the very existence of the personal in the teachings of the Authentic Self model:

> "In fact, if you step back, you realize that the very capacity to experience that personal drama of 'me' has been produced by this vast process" (p. 149).

> "*So even the fact that experience appears to be personal is an impersonal evolutionary phenomenon*" (p. 149, emphasis in original).

> "I'm not denying that your experience *feels* personal. Your experience feels personal to you. My experience feels personal to me. The whole point, though, is that even that experience of it feeling personal is completely impersonal" (p. 149, emphasis in original).

> "We are a process. *You are a process*.... Dare to face this and you will become transparent to yourself" (p. 149).

In contrast, the Unique Self teaching views the personal beyond the impersonal, the personal which transcends and includes the impersonal, as a face of the very essence of reality. From the perspective of Unique Self, it is not the personal which is an illusion, but the impersonal. It is not that the impersonal does not exist. It is rather that, in the manifest world, the impersonal never appears without the personal. From the perspective of deep reality consideration, we realize that, in fact, there is no impersonal self anywhere in the manifest world and that perspective is an irreducible feature of essence. In the Authentic Self teaching, perspective is not irreducible, but is rather a function of conditioning.

As Nagarjuna already pointed out in his critique of the classical enlightenment teachings of Theravada (Theravadan Buddhism is co-emergent and parallel in many respects to the Advaita Vedanta perspective so clearly informing the Authentic Self teaching), there is no emptiness without form and no form without emptiness. We add to that ancient realization of enlightenment the irreducible ontology of perspectives, which modernity and postmodernity have realized so profoundly and which Integral theory has placed front and center. All form has perspective, and that refers not only to the form of personal ego, but to all form, all the way up and all the way down. Your enlightenment has a perspective. Enlightenment always has a perspective, which is your personal perspective. A dimension of that perspective is conditioned by the variables at play in level-one personal. However, perspective is ultimately prior to conditioning and remains even after the evolutionary transcendence beyond conditioning. Emptiness, to borrow the Buddhist use of the term, is never free from form, which includes the personal perspective of the unique set of eyes that are looking through True Self. This is precisely what we have called Unique Self enlightenment. In the quote below, perspective is reduced to an "outer sheath," part of the "conditioned" "personal," which, as we have already seen, is always "secondary."

> "... the same singularity that is looking at the world through the prism of the conditioned perspective of a particular body and mind. And all of the attributes of that body and mind—its biological nature, its ethnic and cultural background, its personal history and its emotional and psychological tendencies—are like *outer sheaths*" (pgs. 149-50, emphasis added).

In this understanding, perspective is reduced to conditioning and relegated to the outer sheath. Unique Self points out that the impersonal always sees through a unique set of eyes and is, therefore, never devoid of the personal. Unique cannot be reduced to the conditioning of ego that must be overcome. While a dimension of uniqueness is certainly a function of conditioning, uniqueness is no less a quality of essence.[49]

What the Unique Self teaching shares with the Authentic Self teaching is the instruction to have the personal see through the perspective of the impersonal:

> "When you authentically transcend the ego's personal drama and discover the truth of the impersonal process, the personal sphere of your life does not cease to exist…. Our experience of the personal sphere is the primary filter through which we see and engage with the world around us…. But if you can see the personal sphere from the perspective of an impersonal cosmic process, there will be *space* around the arising of those impulses" (p. 153).

When that means expanding your perspective to see yourself in a larger evolutionary context, Unique Self fully affirms that aspect of this teaching. This is core to the realization of what I have called the Evolutionary Unique Self. But in the Authentic Self teaching, these citations are part of a much broader and sustained devaluation and degradation of the personal.

Authentic Self seeks a more definitive split between the personal and impersonal, which are identified explicitly as the relative and the absolute, as in the following quote:

> "For example, we tend to think of ourselves as individuals with a unique personality based upon some combination of our psychological experience, our ethnic identity, our cultural background, our gender, and our personal strengths and talents…. While these are real and valid aspects of ourselves, they are all relative because they are only partial.

---

49 In many expressions of non-dual teaching, the entire distinction between conditioning and beyond conditioning, the absolute and the relative, needs to be re-considered. Strangely enough, powerful non-dual teaching seems to virtually always draw a sharply dual line in the sand between the relative and the absolute.

There is, however, another dimension altogether upon which we can base our sense of identity, a dimension that is radically different from all others because its very nature is non-relative or absolute" (pgs. 60-61).

The personal and the unique are mistakenly identified in this passage and in many others with the relative.

There is, in actuality, a perpetual dance between the personal and impersonal. Personal ethics and utopian ethics are always held in grand dialectical tension, which is constantly moving toward higher integration and alignment. For an individual, the failure to recognize and hold this dialectical tension results in either personal narcissism or various shades of impersonal alienation "for the sake of the all." In the unfolding of the spiritual path, this dialectical dance between personal and impersonal is ever-present. The core movements in this dance are the essential stages of evolution. Unique Self holds preciously the paradoxical dialectic between the personal and the impersonal. From a genuine non-dual perspective, holiness is in paradox, not paradise. Dialectical tension is essential for integrity. For Lainer, a defining characteristic of liberated consciousness, i.e., of non-dual humanism, is the ability to maintain paradox.[50]

DISTINCTION FIVE: SEPARATE AND UNIQUE

In the Authentic Self teachings, separateness, as in the sense of the Separate Self, is routinely conflated with uniqueness, and both are identified with the small self and the personal at the limited level of egoic consciousness:

"This shift of perspective enables us to powerfully penetrate the walls of our separate, personal existence" (p. 146).

"The separate self-sense is nothing more than an illusion of uniqueness, created moment by moment through our

---

50   See Radical Kabbalah (Gafni, 2012) for the full discussion of laughter and paradox in Unique Self consciousness.

compulsive habit of personalizing almost every thought, feeling, and sensation we have" (p. 148).

The personal self—which this teaching confuses with the small self of the ego—is dismissed as an illusion that needs to be dispelled with the realization that there is no self, but only a process. We have already discussed this distinction in part in Distinction One: "The Awakened Personal and Impersonal Function," which focused on the level one / level three fallacy. That is to say, the distinction addresses the confusion between personal at the level of ego and the personal at the level of Unique Self.

In *Your Unique Self,* I spend a critical chapter drawing the all-important distinction between separateness and uniqueness. To awaken to True Self is to realize that we all participate in the seamless coat of the universe. It is to realize that you are not apart and not separate. However, the seamless coat of the universe is seamless, not featureless. You are its unique features. Uniqueness is not merely a property of ego. It is a property of essence.

Both Eastern and Western thought confused separateness and uniqueness.

The Essential Discernment Between Separateness and Uniqueness

Perhaps the greatest mistake in the evolution of human spirituality was the failure to properly distinguish between separateness and uniqueness. This simple statement is the result of many years of meditation on Unique Self and the reading of countless classic and popular texts that all confused separateness and uniqueness, each in its own way. Once this realization dawned on me, I could see that one of the great intractable problems standing in the face of human evolution could be resolved. The knotted contradiction between the major types of human spirituality are easily unraveled, opening the door to a higher Integral embrace of enlightenment. This acknowledgment of the difference between separate and unique in turn allows us to move one vital step closer toward the emergence of a genuine translineage dharma and World Spirituality.

The core contradiction lies between the dominant motifs and moods of Eastern and Western spirituality.

Each suggests a different path—paths that are, to a large extent, mutually exclusive. Both are right and both are wrong. Or to put it another way, each one has a piece of the story, but each thinks its respective piece is actually the whole story. *When a part pretends to be a whole, pathology of some form is invariably produced.* Moreover, Eastern and Western spirituality each make a critical mistake based on an essential confusion between separateness and uniqueness.

Each side in this dharma combat, which has spanned the generations, is motivated by pure and holy motives. Each, with its teachings and practices, seeks the highest expression and flowering of human love and goodness. Each, with its teachings and practices, wishes to end suffering. Yet each made the same mistake, in the opposite manner.

The Insight and Mistake of the East

Eastern spirituality by and large rightly sees the separate self as an illusion. The realization of this illusion comes from profound spiritual practices like meditation, which work to open the eye of the spirit. Not only is the separate self exposed as an illusion, it is also the root source of most human suffering. Fear, death, terror, and cruelty in virtually all of its forms can ultimately be traced back to the illusion of the separate self. It is for this most powerful and compelling of reasons that the East devoted an enormous amount of energy to dispelling the illusion of the separate ego self.

In realizing that the separate self is an illusion, the East made a mistake: it confused separateness and uniqueness. The axiomatic assumption in many Eastern teachings—both ancient and modern—is that to transcend the separate self, you must leave behind not only the illusion of separation, but also the apparent experience of uniqueness.

Much effort was directed to demonstrating that what seemed to be unique and particular was in fact common and universal, and what seemed to be personal was actually impersonal. There was great truth in some of this teaching, and it clearly brought immense spiritual depth and some measure of peace to many.

And yet the core teaching did not take root among the masses. The problem was not simply that the masses were lazy, stupid, or in lower states of consciousness, as some teachers told us. The deeper problem was that the masses felt that the teaching violated their basic sense of the necessity, desirability, and dignity of uniqueness. The problem was—and is—that uniqueness will just not go away. The majority of people correctly and intuitively feel that to surrender their uniqueness would be to surrender their life force, as well as their personal value and dignity. The personal is, by its very nature, *unique*. The dignity and value of the personal derive directly from its uniqueness.

You can have a powerful and authentic experience of your own specialness even after the dissolution of your ego. Many Eastern teachings try valiantly to explain this away by telling you in many different ways that your lingering experience of uniqueness or specialness is merely evidence that you have not yet evolved beyond ego.[51]

But you, and many like you, know in your deepest place that this is simply not true. You experience the reality of your specialness and uniqueness not as an expression of ego, but as a glorious expression of your truest nature. *You understand that the seamless coat of the Uni-verse is indeed seamless, but not featureless. You understand that your uniqueness is the highest expression of God looking out from behind your eyes and taking in your uniquely gorgeous perspective and insight.* You must move beyond your separate self, even as you must embrace and affirm your uniqueness beyond ego. Because the East demands that you throw out your uniqueness as part of dispelling the illusion of the ego or the separate self, you correctly rebel against this dharma. You intuitively affirm the value of the personal. To you, impersonality feels like a violation of the very quality of humanness that you hold most dear.

You feel your uniqueness as a deep truth. So you reject the dharma of the East, and while trying to salvage your uniqueness, you cling to your separate self. What other choice do you have?

---

51 For a response to this type of critique of Unique Self see the endnotes to this volume.

This non-choice is the result of the conflation of separateness and uniqueness. Ironically, the failure of popular perceptions of virtually all Eastern approaches to spirituality to make this essential distinction between uniqueness and separateness undermines the ability of the discerning heart and mind to receive the great dharma of the East. It is for this reason that the Eastern teachings that have been disseminated throughout the Western world have ultimately failed to break out of a very small and elite audience, and have not had a genuinely transformative impact upon mainstream culture.

Of course the East is half right. The illusion of an isolated ego, the separate self, really is the source of so much of our suffering. And yet, the confusion between separateness and uniqueness in Eastern teaching has paradoxically caused the rejection of Eastern teaching in the West. The West has essentially ignored the Eastern call to evolve beyond separate-self ego, and most of humanity has remained stuck with ego and all of its attendant horrors.[52]

The Insight and Mistake of the West

Conventional Western spirituality, like the spirituality of the East, is motivated by love and the desire to end suffering. However, the West came to essentially opposite conclusions about how to achieve this same result. The West saw the affirmation of human individuality as the greatest good of the human spirit. Western spirituality asserted that our rights and relationships are rooted in the dignity of the separate self. It is the separate self that is in relationship not only with others, but also with God. Communion

---

52 Mysticism particularly, but not only, of the Eastern variety made a second critical mistake. It failed to distinguish between what Integral theory refers to as states and stages. States refer to states of expanded or distorted consciousness, while stages refer to distinct levels of developmental consciousness. State development, from separate to True Self, is insufficient to heal suffering. This was a core mistake of Eastern mysticism. We also need structure-stage development to higher levels of consciousness from mythic rational to pluralistic to second-tier. "State development" refers to the process of waking up to your True Nature. "Stage-structure development" refers to the process of growing up to higher levels of consciousness—for example, growth from egocentric to ethnocentric to world-centric consciousness.

with the divine rather than absorption into the One becomes the good of spiritual practice.

It is the great divine gift to affirm human adequacy and dignity through the very encounter between humans and God. For humans to be addressed in this encounter, their distinct otherness as a separate self apart from God must be affirmed and supported. In other words, our relationship with God requires some degree of separation. *Two parties can only meet in love and mutuality if they are separate.* We are both overwhelmed by the presence and at the same time affirmed by the presence as a separate other. In the revelation of the infinite, the finite is held in love, nourished and challenged at the same time. *Our individuality becomes the source of our dignity. Moreover, it is in our individuality that we find our ability to love, to act in compassion, and to take responsibility for our destiny.*

For one who is wholly merged with the infinite, there is no Encounter. If there is no Encounter, then there is no love, no dignity, and no responsibility. If there is no other, then we cease to be a moral agent and a lover. With the total annihilation of the personal comes the end of personal responsibility. If human beings are not separate selves with individual rights and responsibilities, then there is neither good nor evil. It becomes virtually impossible to distinguish between what is below and what is beyond. Good and evil imply relationship. When there is an identity of subjects, when humans and God are one, when we are truly submerged in a condition of *tat tvam asi* ("Thou Art That"), there can be no relationship. Where there is no relationship, there is no love, no good, and no evil.

The miracle of We comes only from the union of I and Thou. What is love without an I and a Thou? Ethics, goodness, and judgment are meaningful only in the realm of the personal. They have no place in a Uni-verse of no-selves.

For all of these very noble reasons, the West insisted on the reality of the separate self as the essential human identity. However, Western spirituality made the same great mistake as the East, but in the opposite direction. The West essentially confused separateness and uniqueness. Western teachers wrongly assumed that all the virtues of love and relationship required the dignity of individuality in the form of a separate self. This is simply not true. All the goods and virtues of love, relationship, compassion, responsibility, and all the rest can be had through the Unique Self. There is absolutely no need for the separate self as the essential human identity. *The Unique Self, as we have shown, emerges in its full splendor only after the separate self has been trance-ended.* You can experience the full dignity, responsibility, and joy of individuality by recognizing your uniqueness. Uniqueness does not require separateness.

The result of this colossal mistake in Western spirituality has been that your intuitive spiritual desire to evolve beyond exclusive identification with your ego—to transcend your separate self—has been thwarted and even ridiculed by Western spiritual teaching. Your desire to reach for the transpersonal was stymied because it seemed like you needed to reject the personal to get there. The Western deification of the personal blocked the gateways necessary for your enlightenment.[53] Your heart knew this was wrong. You knew you needed to transcend your separate self, but you did not know how to do it without losing the critical moral and relational virtues of the personal. So you remained stuck in the personal, unable to find a path beyond yourself.

For both East and West, drawing a correct distinction between separateness and uniqueness allows for a powerful evolution of their respective teachings. This crucial dharmic distinction allows for a higher and Integral embrace of these seemingly disparate teachings, which split the world of spirit into two warring camps.

The Unique Self is the pivot point for this translineage spiritual breakthrough, which allows for the evolutionary integration of these two teachings.

For the West, the Unique Self is the source of human dignity, love, obligation, and destiny. At the deepest level, you know that

---

53 Particularly the failure of western culture to distinguish between what I have termed level one personal—before contact with the transcendent and level two personal—post contact with the transcendent. In our terms, Level 2 is between personal at the level of ego and personal at the level of Unique Self.

your Unique Self is not your separate self. Your separate self, as the sum total of your identity, is an illusion, though you remain a unique strand in the seamless coat of the Uni-verse. *Spiritual practice moves you to realize your essential enmeshment with the larger reality, even as you retain the dignity of your distinction.* Uniqueness is the source of this dignity, as well as your sense of intimacy.

For the East, the realization of Unique Self is equally critical. It is precisely the recognition of the Unique Self that allows for the transcendence of the illusion of separate self without the wholesale rejection of individual specialness and uniqueness. You are able to fully embrace the call to evolve beyond separate self and ego, realizing True Self, even as you affirm and embrace your Unique Self that emerges from your Buddha nature.

For both the East and the West, higher translineage integration can be achieved. A genuine evolution of spirit can be accomplished. The full glory of meditative realization and classic enlightenment is redeemed and recognized as the first major step. In the second step, the full glory of individual dignity is realized in the post-egoic Unique Self.

This distinction between separate and unique is not only cognitive. The realization of uniqueness beyond conditioning is a realization. In the classic formula of Unique Self theory, True Self +perspective=Unique Self. It is a particular world space of enlightenment that can only be accessed directly. This is the core intuition and an utterly correct assertion of Integral semiotics. To state it as succinctly as possible: There is no True Self without a unique perspective, which is but a signifier for the personal. Postmodernism has correctly pointed out that the signifier and the signified are interdependent. That means simply that the words strawberry ice cream are meaningless if one cannot access the world space which tastes strawberry ice cream.

Every world space is accessed through its own enactments or practices. One cannot access the truth of quantum mechanics without mathematical equations, even as one cannot access God without the practices needed to enter that particular world space. The world space once entered will, of course, be mediated through all of the relative contexts that mediate every world space. If one cannot access quantum mechanics because one does not know how or refuses to do the math, but denies its validity, this denial is not taken seriously. Strangely, however, if one denies the ability to access quantum mechanics because one does not know how to access it or one refuses to do the practices that allow one to access that world space, superficial culture takes that seriously. Much of culture itself has forgotten how to access the world space we call God. Not only, however, has culture forgotten, but culture has forgotten that it has forgotten. The same is true of the personal beyond the impersonal. This is a world space that needs to be contacted directly through interior practice or revelation. If a teacher or school of thought has never experienced it, they will tend to say it does not exist. Their natural move will be to conflate the personal with the personality, the separate self or ego self, and not to realize the personal beyond the impersonal, the personal face of essence which is Unique Self.

This is perhaps part of the reason that the Authentic Self teachings seem to incorrectly conflate this level of personal, which transcends and includes the impersonal, with the personal before enlightenment again and again. This is a classic form of what Integral theory has labeled the "pre-trans fallacy."[54] In most of Integral theory, the pre-trans fallacy applies to the confusion between the pre-personal and the transpersonal. Here, the same core fallacy applies to the inappropriate conflation of the personal before the realization of the impersonal and the personal quality that emerges after the realization of enlightenment. The result is that the realization of Unique Self is consistently denied. This amounts to a denial of reality, for there is simply no impersonal without the personal, no True Self without Unique Self, no emptiness without form, and no form without uniqueness. Again and again, in *Evolutionary Enlightenment*, separateness is confused with uniqueness, which is relegated to the realm of the personal. Again and again, Unique Self is rejected:

---

54 See K. Wilber (1980) for more on the pre/trans fallacy.

"From the perspective of Evolutionary Enlightenment, *you* are very important. Not your individual qualities, your unique personality, or your particular gifts and talents. What makes you important is that you have the capacity to directly awaken to the fact that who you are is not separate from the energy and intelligence that created the universe" (p. 77).

The process is always identified with liberation and enlightenment, while the personal is identified with compulsive habit or narcissism—that is to say, with the personal at the level of small self:

> Liberation is when we see "every aspect of our human experience as part and parcel of the vast impersonal cosmic process," which "enables us to break through the habit of compulsive personalization" (p. 145).

> "[W]e discover the liberating truth that life is not a personal drama but is in fact an impersonal process" (p. 146).

> "As you see through the illusion of the personal, you will recognize the truth that who we are as human beings is a bundle of impulses, reactions, and habits, conditioned patterns that together create the convincing appearance of unique individuality" (p. 149).

This, according to these teachings, is what we need to overcome—seeing the self as a "unique entity," which is somehow special.

The confusion in Authentic Self theory between level-one personal ego self and uniqueness keeps repeating itself:

> "But if we want to evolve, it's imperative to recognize, at least momentarily, the radical arbitrariness of these differences that we consider to be so personal and so meaningful" (p. 150).

"It takes courage and humility to let in how much of what you consider to be uniquely you has actually been shaped by the evolutionary process and the world around you" (p. 151).

"As you see through the illusion of the personal, you will recognize the truth that who we are as human beings is a bundle of impulses, reactions, and habits, conditioned patterns that together create the convincing appearance of unique individuality" (p. 149).

"These many sheaths of identity are usually so close to our felt sense of self that it can be enormously challenging to disembed our awareness from their familiar and habitual viewpoints" (p. 150).

To be enlightened is to deeply grasp the liberating truth that you are not a "personal drama" but an "impersonal process," to get over "the ego's conditioned habit of personalization" (p. 151 and 152).

The ego = personal = separate self = uniqueness = illusion is the core formula which is repeated time and again in *Evolutionary Enlightenment*. This teaching, while profoundly useful as a means of dis-identifying with the egoic self, ultimately suffers from several major flaws. The two most glaring flaws are false conflation of separateness and uniqueness and the devaluation of the personal. The point, which is hammered home repeatedly, is that your essence is not personal. You are a process. You are a cog in the process whose essence is impersonal and therefore virtually, by definition, replaceable. By contrast, the essence of the Unique Self teaching is the irreplaceability of the individual whose infinite dignity and adequacy derives from their irreducible uniqueness. It is hard to imagine a more significant distinction.

"But from the Process Perspective, *none* of it is personal" (p. 149).

"We awaken to the radically impersonal nature of the very event of experience itself..." (p. 149).

"[T]he ego likes to create the illusion" that your life "is a personal affair" (p. 149).

"The narcissistic separate self creates the appearance of a personal drama with you at center stage. But it's not actually real" (p. 149).

Again, the devaluation of the personal is consistent and withering. Uniqueness is virtually never used as a positive term in all of the key discussions of enlightenment in the book. Without this overall sense of what the book is saying, each individual quote would be innocuous, similar to many quotes of this nature in the enlightenment literature. However, when placed in context, they become part of the dismissal of uniqueness; the equation of the unique, separate, and personal; and occasional apologetics notwithstanding, the core devaluation of the personal.[55]

DISTINCTION SIX: SPECIAL OR NOT SPECIAL?

A sixth distinction between the Authentic and Unique Self teaching is their respective approaches to the personal issue of Specialness. Authentic Self teaching states clearly:

> "There is nothing more powerful than this Process Perspective to help us see through the seductive veil of narcissism that has become our personal and cultural predicament" (p. 148).

It is difficult to transcend this because "[most of us have been brought up to believe that we are unique individuals, that we are special, that there is nobody quite like us" (p. 148).

---

55 Moreover, as in the following citation, in Authentic Self teaching, process and personal are set up as dualistic opposites rather than as living in the paradoxical dialectical relationship, which is core to the Unique Self model.

The distinction between "specialness" at the level of ego and "specialness" at the level of Unique Self, which is core to the Unique Self teaching, is absent in the Authentic Self teaching. From an objective and subjective Unique Self perspective, you realize correctly that you are special, and there is nobody quite like you.

One of the most confusing things to people on a genuine spiritual path is the utter denial of specialness. You have an experience that you are special, but you are told by spiritual teachers and books that if you experience yourself as special, you are still stuck in ego. So, you work really hard to get rid of the feeling of being special. But it is always there, lurking in the corner just beneath the surface of your spiritual posturing. This makes you feel like an impostor and fraud. On the one hand, you are having intense spiritual experiences during regular practice, and you are living your compassion in the world. On the other hand, the lurking feeling of specialness makes you believe your realization is false and fraudulent. "Special" is often used interchangeably with "unique." To think you are special is to think you are unique, which is radically rejected by most spiritual teachers on the contemporary scene.

Authentic Self teachings regularly speak of "the illusion of uniqueness." A cornerstone of these teachings of impersonal enlightenment is that there is "no such thing as a unique spiritual experience." This is precisely wrong. The deeper the spiritual experience, the more unique it becomes. In fact, there is no such thing as a non-unique spiritual experience. Your enlightenment always has a perspective. The very essence of enlightenment is the liberation of your unique perspective from the prison of voices not your own.

A second example of this rejection of specialness as belonging only to the realm of the ego self from popular enlightenment teachings is found in *A Course in Miracles*. Below is a citation from one entry, entitled "The Pursuit of Specialness":

> *The pursuit of Specialness*
> *is always at the cost of peace.*
> *You are not Special.*

If you think you are
and would defend your specialness
against the truth of what you really are,
how can you know the truth?
Specialness always makes comparisons.
It is established by a lack seen in another.
The pursuit of Specialness
must bring you pain.[56]

The conclusion of the section is that specialness is but an illusion that needs to be forgiven and dispelled through forgiveness.

A Course in Miracles is a significant and profound teaching. And yet in both examples and in the larger teachings that they represent, the same two mistakes are made. First, there is a complete conflation of uniqueness or specialness on the one side and separateness on the other. They are all taken to refer to the same thing. Now, it is true that the assertion of specialness is one of the favorite tactics through which the consciousness of separate self attempts to ward off the terror of its own inevitable death and dissolution. From this perspective, specialness is indeed an illusion of ego to be overcome in order to gain the peace and joy that come from a realization of your True Nature, the realization that you are not separate or alone, but are an indivisible and eternal expression of the seamless coat of the Uni-verse. However, from the perspective of Unique Self, of course, you are special. That is precisely what it means to be a Unique Self. Your utter uniqueness is precisely what makes you special.

The second confusion in the teaching that blithely rejects specialness is the failure to distinguish between different levels of

---

56 A well-known popularizer of the Course in Miracles Marianne Williamson fails to distinguish between specialness, or uniqueness, at the level of ego and Unique Self in citing this passage. Indeed no such distinction is made in this passage. See M. Williamson (1996). *Return to Love: A Reflection on the Principles of a Course in Miracles*. New York: Harper Collins, pp. 110. I believe the Course in Miracles itself ultimately does make this distinction and actually brings specialness back on line at the level of Unique Self. See chapter 25 of *Your Unique Self* on the Special function. I thank Roger Walsh and Angela Rutten for this reference.

consciousness. When you are operating from the level of ego, your feeling that "I am special" is the ego's delusion. The ego's feeling that "I am special" is based on something unreal. Seduced by the significance of this truth, enlightenment teachers who stress dis-identification with ego will often mistakenly conflate personal-specialness with ego-specialness, and therefore, wrongly reject specialness and personal uniqueness altogether.

Eastern-influenced teachers of evolution beyond ego correctly point out that most of the experiences that you feel are special and personal are really, at their core, shockingly impersonal. You think, for example, that all of your sexing is intimate and personal to you, when in fact, much of your sexing can be said to result from a vast, impersonal sexual current that courses through you and everyone else on the planet. Or, to take another example, you think that these details of your life are all very special, personal, and fascinating, when in fact they are very common, ordinary, and even banal. Ninety-five percent of your waking thoughts are dedicated to reviewing details of old stories and worrying about how new stories will play out. You get lost in personality and miss essence. Much of what you thought was personal is actually impersonal.

This move beyond the obsession with the personal helps you to wake up. You evolve from separate self to True Self. You begin to realize that you are in fact not an isolated or separate part, but rather you are part of the whole, of All-That-Is. The problem is that, for most enlightenment paths, this is the end of the road, which is a mistake. Once, however, you have had a True Self realization or even a glimmer of that realization, the personal will begin to come back online at a higher level. At this point, your Unique Self, your feeling of specialness, reemerges, but this time in a far cleaner, clearer, and more crystalline form. As my lineage master Mordechai Lainer of Izbica taught, when you evolve beyond ego, your uniqueness/specialness does not disappear; it becomes clarified. At the Unique Self level of consciousness, you reconnect to your specialness with the stunning realization: You are special! You are unique!

There are many differences between egoic specialness and Unique Self specialness, which emerge in moments of evolution beyond exclusive identification with ego. But one distinction stands out as a surefire litmus test that will always allow you to distinguish between egoic and Unique Self specialness: specialness at the level of ego is always at someone else's expense. If I am special, that means that others are not. This is the level of ego that *A Course in Miracles* was referring to in saying that specialness exists only by comparison. However, specialness at the level of Unique Self is of a different order of reality. Unique Self specialness is an authentic realization of overpowering joy. I am special, and so are you. Each of us has a Unique Self. We are not equally talented, wise, sensual, or compassionate. But paradoxically, we are all special, each in our own infinitely unique ways. In the enlightened identification of your Uniqueness, you realize your specialness, which is a wondrous and gorgeous expression of your very enlightenment. It is paradoxically this very realization that opens you up to fully perceive and delight in the specialness of others.

DISTINCTION SEVEN: AUTHENTIC SELF, UNIQUE SELF, AND THE PERSONAL FACE OF GOD

In many passages in *Evolutionary Enlightenment* and in other related Authentic Self teachings, there is an explicit and implicit rejection of the personal God:

> "But the truth is that *there isn't anybody in there.* Or, another way of looking at this same picture would be that there is only One in there. And that One, the 'I' of the cosmos, is … the same singularity that is looking at the world through the prism of the conditioned perspective of a particular body and mind. And all of the attributes of that body and mind—its biological nature, its ethnic and cultural background, its personal history and its emotional and psychological tendencies—are like **outer sheaths**" (pgs. 149-50, emphasis added).

"There is no God principle that stands outside or beyond the self, it is completely dependent on human beings..." ("Awakening Your Authentic Self," Audio, *EnlightenNext*, 2009.)

By contrast, Unique Self implies relationship. Irreducible uniqueness creates the face of the other that yearns to recognize and be recognized. Mutual recognition is realized in the face-to-face relationship. For Unique Self, the paradoxical encounter with the second person of God is not dogma, but realization. Sufi master Rumi and Hasidic master Levi Isaac of Berdichev do not "believe" in the personal god. Rather, they know and taste the personal face of essence. Unique Self is paradoxically the unique expression of God in the first-person, what the *Upanishads* called, Thou Art That, known in Buddhism as I Amness, even as it clearly implies God in the second-person, the unique face-to-face encounter of other with Source. At the same time, Unique Self incarnates God in the third person, the conscious and unique expression of the evolutionary impulse, God having a You experience. Therefore, it would be most correct to say that in Unique Self realization, the three faces of God incarnate in paradoxical unity. This is the holy trinity that lies at the core of Unique Self.

What I have termed Evolutionary Unique Self is the personal face of the process living in you, as you, and through you. Awakening to the process uniquely expressed as you is the core of Unique Self enlightenment. But first person must always live in dialectical and seamless tension with second person. One bows to second person, even as one is indivisibly part of the second person before whom he bows. For the moment, I will focus on the second-face of God to highlight the distinction between the Unique Self and Authentic Self models.

From the perspective of Unique Self, God in second-person communion is an enlightened realization. It is core to what makes our lives worth living. Communion is the movement from loneliness to loving. Communion is the lived personal realization of being held and received. It is the core realization of the great Sufi mystics and the essence of Rumi's poetry of enlightenment. It is the experience, to cite my lineage master Mordechai Lainer of Izbica, that "every place you fall, you fall into God's hands." From the perspective of Unique Self, evolutionary responsibility is an intensely personal affair. We are all systematically misrecognized. To be recognized is to be seen. To be seen is to be loved. To be loved is to be in communion. It is only when we are seen that we are called to the fullness of our glimmering beauty as unique incarnations of the divine treasure. It is only when we are seen that we feel called by the personal evolutionary impulse that lives in us to give the Unique gifts that are only ours to give and that are desperately desired by All-That-Is. To paraphrase twentieth century philosopher, Abraham Joshua Heschel, to be in communion is to know that your deed is God's need. Heschel famously and appropriately called this teaching Divine Pathos. It is the path of the lover pining for the beloved. It is, however, not a new or original teaching. Rather Heschel himself is a direct scion of the great Hasidic dynasty of Opt, descended from the line of mystical master students of the Baal Shem Tov, and he is simply reformulating the classic kabbalistic teaching of God in the second person. The teaching moves a significant step beyond the biblical notion of God in the second person, or perhaps to state it more clearly, it emerges from the most radical formulation of God in the second person in the Bible, the formulation found in the biblical book, the "Song of Songs." In the "Songs of Songs," attributed traditionally to King Solomon, the human being and God are portrayed as lovers in full erotic pathos and passion. The lovers yearn for each other and need each other. This is the source of the titles of key Heschel books, including *God in Search of Man* and *Man in Search of God*.

It is the realization of communion that gives us joy and calls us to evolutionary responsibility.

In this sense as well, Unique Self and Authentic Self teachings diverge. For Unique Self, the call to evolutionary awakening is intimately personal and enacted, at least in part, by the call[57] of God in the second person.[58]

"Communion" is the name that Kabbalah scholar Gershom Scholem gave to the experience of God in the second person. This is the inner experience of a human being who is not merged with the divine, but rather stands in relation to God. This state of relatedness to God is the essence of Hebrew biblical consciousness. According to Scholem, it defines Hebrew mystical consciousness as well. God in second person is all about relationship—whether it is the relationship of a servant to his master, a lover to her beloved, a relationship with a partner, or even a relationship with a friend. All of these can be ways of "relating" to God, and all of these models of relationship find expression in Hebrew wisdom teachings. All are ways of approaching God in the second person.

Nachman of Bratzlav taught the spiritual practice of *Hitbodedut*. In one form, this meant walking alone in the forest "talking to God as you would to your friend." This is the God of prayer. The God of prayer is not a concept, but a realization. I recall a recent conversation with a well-known Buddhist teacher. He said to me, "How can a serious teacher like you believe in the dogma of prayer?" I asked him, "How can you believe in the dogma of awareness?" He said to me, "Awareness is not a dogma; it is a realization," to which I responded, "Yes, of course it is. And so is prayer." With God in the second person, we meet God and bow. With God in the second person, we meet God and partner. With God in the second person, we meet God and love. With God in the second person, we meet God and pray. The key to experiencing God in the second person is the encounter. It is the encounter with God in history and in the lived reality of every human being that is the essence of the God in the second person experience.

This teacher later told me that this simple pointing-out instruction shifted his entire relationship to prayer. Prayer is not

---

57 The Unique Self is called by evolutionary potential and calls us to our evolution.

58 See G. Scholem (1971) famous essay on communion, in his collection of essay entitled *The Messianic Idea*.

a dogma. It is a realization of God in the second person. It is the felt sense that every place you fall, you fall into God's hands. Not the God of the mythic, ethnocentric church or synagogue or mosque or temple. Not that God. Not the God that as a modern or postmodern skeptic, you do not believe in. The God you don't believe in does not exist! Rather, God in second person is the personal face of Essence. It is the aspect of personal Essence that knows your name and cares about every detail of your life.

Feel into the quality of the personal that lives in you, as you, and through you. Remember, perhaps, a time when you felt alienated in a relationship, and you said to your partner, "I feel you are being so impersonal." Or remember a time when you critiqued some dimension of society as being too impersonal. Inherently, you sensed that Essence has a personal quality. This personal Essence is beyond the grasping of the skin-encapsulated ego, which still believes itself to be separate from All-That-Is. It is rather the personal quality of Source. As I was preparing the final draft of this book, my dear friend Annie said to me, "I am a pantheist. I have no access or interest in the second person. God is a crutch for the weak and a dogma of the old religions." Annie just had a beautiful daughter, lovebeing. I asked her to feel into the quality of personal love with which she held lovebeing and then to ask herself the question: Is this quality of the personal sourced in you? Or is it sourced in a deeper, larger quality of the personal from which you draw? She was easily able to sense that the latter must be the case. She was able to "trace the personal back to its source." I told her, "In the same way that you are holding lovebeing—your daughter, Annie—you are being held by the personal face of all-that-is, that knows your name, and that cares infinitely about you."

Unique Self implies prayer, or what Buber called the I-thou relation. It is told that when Hassidic master Levi Yitzchak of Berditchev used to pray, he would begin to say the standard liturgical form of blessing, "Baruch Atah, Adonai," "Blessed are you, God." Then, he would break out of the formal mode of blessing, crying out in sheer joy, "YOU... YOU...YOU ...YOU!" He would lose himself in these words, repeatedly shouting in ecstasy,

"YOU... YOU... YOU!!!" This is the rapture of God in the second person. For Levi Yitzchak, the blessing is what the Buddhists call a "pointing-out instruction." But the words point not to *sunyata* or emptiness, but to God as a beloved Other.

Levi Isaac of Berdichev in the story above did not faint in ecstasy because he was moved by the *dogma* of a personal God. Rather, he fainted in ecstasy at the *felt experience and realization* of the lived encounter, in that very moment, with the personal face of God. It is the experience of God in the second person that inspires prayer. The following is a transcript completed by a student of mine following a private student session in the Holy of Holies on this topic:

> A true story for you today... beloved, Elizabeth Helen.
>
> I once had lunch with a beautiful man who was a famous Buddhist teacher. He said to me, "Marc, I hear you are a great teacher with a beautiful transmission, but I cannot take you seriously."
>
> "Why I asked?" taking mock offense.
>
> He said, "Because I understand that you believe in prayer."
>
> I said to him, "I don't believe in prayer, I know prayer." And, then I said to him, "What do you know?"
>
> "I know awareness," he said.
>
> "You mean you believe in awareness?" I asked.
>
> He said, "No, I know awareness. Awareness isn't a dogma, awareness is a realization."
>
> "Aha, my friend," I responded to him, "Know that prayer is a realization."
>
> His heart opened. We were silent for several long moments. I said to him, "You know now my friend, perhaps for the first time in your life, that every place you fall, you fall into God's hands. . .
>
> "That the God you don't believe in doesn't exist. . .
>
> "That God is not merely the infinity of power, but the infinity of intimacy. . .
>
> "And that you are God's unique intimacy, radically recognized, wildly loved, and fully held."

Our eyes locked, God seeing God, even as we were both held ... by God.[59]

Just as belief in prayer is not a dogma, prayer is not an act of dogma or a religious obligation. True prayer is the ecstatic realization of God in the second person. Prayer is an expression of the radically personal nature of enlightenment--the place in which the personal Unique Self talks to the personal God.

To truly understand and embody the interior face of Essence, one needs to move through three core levels of consciousness. Level One occurs when the Pre-personal emerges as the Personal Self. This is the important level of separate self, ego, and personality. Level Two is when the personal—in a healthy and non-dissociative process—is transcended and included into the impersonal. This is the classic state of enlightenment, which appears in all the great traditions. The personal is trance-ended. You end the trance of the personal self and realize that you are part of the vast impersonal Essence of All-That-Is. It is impersonal in the sense that is beyond the individual personality of any one person. It is the seamless coat of the universe of which you are a part.

However, that is not the end of the story. The seamless coat of the universe is seamless, but not featureless. Some of its features are expressed uniquely as your personal incarnation of Essence. Your irreducible uniqueness is an expression of the personal quality of the divine, beyond the impersonal. In this stage of development, the impersonal then reveals its personal face. You experience the personal face of the vast impersonal divine Essence that suffuses, animates, and embodies All-That-Is. This is level three. Level one is personal, level two impersonal, and level three personal again. When the personal comes back online, it is not the level one personal before the impersonal, but a higher level of personal, what I have termed the level two personal beyond the impersonal.

---

59 Holy of Holies with Marc Gafni, December, 2013. Transcribed by Adael Elizabeth Helen Bullock.

In prayer, the personhood of God meets the personhood of a human being. Prayer is the flight of the lonely one to the Lonely One. Or, as Hassidic master Ephraim of Sudykov said, it is the meeting of misunderstood man with misunderstood God. Human being and God meet, realizing that they are both strangers in the land. They end up in a friendship in which both are liberated and redeemed from loneliness.[60] We are used to thinking of Essence in impersonal terms. In the usual thinking of the spiritual world, the human being has a personality or separate self, which is transcended in enlightenment and melts into the impersonal Essence of All-That-Is. This, however, is only a part of the story. Core to the Unique Self teaching is the realization of personal Essence, which is beyond the impersonal.[5] This is the quality of God in the second person. Here, we are not speaking of a kind of Santa Claus God-in-the-sky. That is merely your personality, or perhaps your mother or father's personhood, writ large! Rather, this personal beyond the impersonal is the personal face of All-That-Is, the aspect of universal Essence that knows your name and cares about your life. It is the divine Mother who holds you in her loving embrace, comforts you, yet challenges you to your greatness at the very same moment,[6] even as you are an indivisible part of her.[61]

The second face of God is the infinity of intimacy, which invites your approach and your prayer. Prayer and intimacy are almost synonymous words. The personal face of Essence, which knows your name, affirms the infinite dignity, value, and adequacy of your personhood, even as prayer affirms the dignity of personal need. Our praise and our petition, our confessions, and even our crying out in need are all addressed to the second person face of God, which is invoked through the enacted technology of prayer. Prayer is, in the teaching of Unique Self, the way of initiating a conversation with, and thereby invoking, the

---

60 See Degal Machaneh Ephraim, 1896, Leviticus 25.
61 For a post-postmodern statement of this form of panentheism, see A. Greene (2010). I am presently writing a review of Greene's work and its relation to justice, narrative, and the primacy of the personal.

infinitely gorgeous face of the personal God, God in the second person. Both prophecy and prayer are natural functions of the Unique Self relation. The difference only is that, in prophecy, God initiates and God invokes, while in prayer, man initiates and man invokes. These are both, however, prophecy and prayer, face-to-face, second-person encounters with Unique Self. This is the type of panentheism that is key to Hasidic discourse.

Not surprisingly, as Moshe Idel has already noted, Levi Isaac, who cried out, "You You You," falling into ecstasy from the potency of his second person realization, is also one of the greatest non-dual first-personal realizers of Hasidism. It's in the paradoxical dialectic between the personal and impersonal—first, second, and third person—that full enlightenment is realized.

This face-to-face dimension of enlightened second personhood is absent in the Authentic Self teachings. Both Authentic Self and Unique Self teaching see God in third person as the impersonal evolutionary impulse. In the Authentic Self teaching, however, to align with this impulse in third person requires leaving the personal behind in any meaningful way. In the Authentic Self teaching, there is no genuine second-person. In Unique Self teaching, the second-person is a lived realization. Naturally then, aligning with God in the third-person, the impersonal evolutionary impulse, does not require a nullification of the personal; rather, it requires a clarification of the personal. The personal is purified of its egoic contraction through contact with the impersonal spaciousness of enlightened consciousness. The personal then emerges again in full radiance as Unique Self. Liberation always requires that we make ourselves transparent to Self. But it also demands that we realize our place in the larger historical evolutionary context. These are two distinct forms of awakening. And, yet, one must never so identify with the process that one loses the felt sense of the infinite value, dignity, and adequacy of oneself as a personal individual and of every single personal individual that one encounters. The dialectical dance of the personal and impersonal must never stop.

DISTINCTION EIGHT: TEACHER AND STUDENT

Unique Self teaching has two major implications in the spiritual context of teacher-student relationships. When teachers give their students only impersonal or kosmic love, even when it is genuine, the students cannot truly grow. Personal love releases the contraction of ego. When the teacher sees the student merely as a seeker whose ego longs for release, something of vital importance is lost in the teacher-student relationship. The student doesn't need to be coddled by the teacher, yet it is absolutely essential for the student to be seen and valued uniquely by the teacher. This is an essential human need. This is what it means to be loved. When this happens, a deep place in the student begins to stir. The student has been seen, and therefore, his/her self- contraction begins to uncoil. The student's ego relaxes its grasping grip, and Unique Self begins to emerge though genuine contact from the Unique Self of the teacher, which further elicits the Unique Self of the student, and vice versa.

The ability to make contact and be intimate or not is the essential distinction between Unique Self and ego. Unique Self can make contact; ego cannot. Many teachers trapped in ego fail to make contact, and therefore, keep their students trapped in ego as well, even if their professed goal is to evolve the student beyond ego to True Self. Why? Because only personal contact releases the contraction of ego.

When the substance of one Unique Self touches the substance of another Unique Self, contact is made. Contact is a touching without ego boundaries and without the loss of the unique individuation of being. One is not "lost in the past," but is totally "present in the now." Presence meets Presence. Both sides have personal history. Both sides of the contact are intensely personal, but neither side is attached to personal history.

When a teacher denies Unique Self by confusing it with egoic uniqueness, and thus views the goal of enlightenment as being the awakening of the impersonal, whether that be realization of oneness with the Ground of Being or alignment with the impersonal evolutionary process, the result is always apparent in the student. The students may be bright, articulate, and all-American. They may say all the right things and look the right way, but at some core level, we cannot make contact with them. We get an uneasy feeling, and we aren't quite sure why. Images of the old movie *The Stepford Wives* come to mind. In this movie, the men of Stepford consider their wives to be nagging, troublesome, egoic, and generally underdeveloped, so the men kill their wives and replace them, in the same body, with wise, wonderful, devoted, mega-sexy, compliant Stepford Wives.[62] The stepford husband in the guise of the teacher often kills the Unique Self by mistaking it for the ego. The authentic divine feminine in both teacher and student has also been killed. What emerges is the student who is the perfect, appropriate, articulate, and clean-cut Stepford Wife—but there is something essentially effaced.

It is because of this that the teacher is obligated to give their students radically personal love, which is the honoring and recognition of the Unique Self of the student. *The recognition of the student's Unique Self releases the student's contraction of ego.* Personal love always releases the contraction of ego. *Personal contact is the joyous essence of being. It can solve world conflicts and create the intimacy that makes life worth living.* When we feel like genuine contact has been made, we have the delightful experience of our Unique Self being received and witnessed. *Like in quantum physics, the process of being seen, in and of itself, evolves us; it invites us into our fullest majesty and reveals our inner splendor.* Unique Self offers a quality of presence that shows up when the ego is set aside, even if temporarily, and our deeper being and becoming emerges in all of its resplendent beauty.

The second implication of Unique Self in the teacher-student relationship is the natural limitation of the authority of the teacher, which is implied by Unique Self, particularly when these

---

62   Both Unique Self and Authentic Self teachings, as in the kind expressed by my colleague Andrew Cohen, would, I believe, agree with this critique of the Stepford Wife student, fostered by a teaching that views True Self as the end goal of the enlightenment process.

teachings are contrasted with other more impersonal constructs of enlightenment. If one experiences that the awakening of self beyond ego is the awakening of an activated and engaged "impersonal" Authentic Self, then the teacher's authority is naturally greater than it might be, according to one who experiences the awakening beyond ego as True Self + perspective, which equals Unique Self. If the goal is impersonal enlightenment, then the teacher who is more realized than the students might naturally assume a powerfully authoritarian approach toward the students. The authority of the teacher is rooted in their having a profoundly higher degree of enlightenment than the student. If this authority is exercised with integrity, then this might be for the benefit of the student. If the authority is exercised in a corrupt manner, then clearly it would not be of benefit to the student. The potential shadow of the impersonal in the teacher-student context may therefore be stated as excessive authority exercised inappropriately.

If, however, the core teaching being used is that of Unique Self, then even if the teacher has natural authority based on a higher degree of realization than the student, the teacher's authority will nonetheless be limited. While the teacher may have a higher level of realization of True Self than the student, by definition the teacher cannot have a higher level of realization of the student's Unique Self for the very reason that the Unique Perspective of the student is not available to the teacher. It may well be the case that the realization of the teacher enables them to see and point to the student's Unique Self more clearly than the student him or herself. However, this pointing out of the student's Unique Self by the teacher must always be held with humility, because the teacher realizes that while their own experience of True Self fully exhausts and transcends that of the student, the same cannot be said for Unique Self. There is an intimate dimension of Unique Self that can never be penetrated by the teacher; hence, the authority of the teacher is naturally limited. The ultimate authority of the student derives from their authorship of their own story, which can never be plagiarized by the teacher.

The potential shadow of the personal Unique Self teacher-student model might be excessive love or intimacy with the student in a context that is inappropriate, abusive or dangerous either to the teacher or the student, or insufficiently demarcated lines of authority between teacher and student. Naturally, the term "excessive" is profoundly subjective. The precise meaning needs to be defined in the space of integrity and love, jointly created by the student and teacher. Intimacy between the powerful adult teacher and student might well be a function of the sincere desire of the teacher to radically hold and love the student. If this happens in the context of a relationship that is not premised on the student's obedience, a powerful and direct love between teacher and student may be a great gift that uncoils the ego and radically holds the student.[63] Intimacy between teacher and student might also be an appropriate beautiful dual relationship between teacher and student in which there is a genuine and mutual love. Or it might be some combination of both. Or it might be an exploitative relationship with the student exploiting the teacher, the teacher taking advantage of the student, or both.

The potential shadow of the various impersonal self teacher-student models might be excessive authority assumed on the part of the teacher, even while sincerely seeking to undermine the egoic structures.

To recapitulate: Authentic Self relationships can foster the shadow of excessive authority. Excessive authority can breed a dynamic that is destructive to both teacher and student. This is not to reject the possible legitimacy and efficacy of authority. It rejects, however, inappropriate authority. What the authority relationship is between teacher and student must be negotiated between them and must be constantly open to revision and evolution.

Unique Self relationships can foster the shadow of inappropriate or dangerous intimacy[7].

---

63 This form of erotic merger is called by the kabbalists *zivug*.

DISTINCTION NINE: UNIQUE SELF, AUTHENTIC SELF, AND RELATIONSHIP TO WOUNDS

In the Authentic Self teachings the point is made time and again that when you awaken to and identify with the process of evolution moving in you, your wounds will not matter so much anymore. The core of this teaching is that when you move beyond the personal to the impersonal, only the process matters. If you just identify with some version of your higher self, you can leave your psychological problems behind. This is a true but partial teaching. It suffers from a number of essential limitations, not least of which is the false split between the personal and the impersonal.

First, let's say what's true about the teaching. If you are living within the narrow identity of your skin-encapsulated ego and you have suffered betrayal or abuse in your life, then it is likely that the pain of these wounds will take up an enormous amount of your psychic space and emotional energy. However, if you have evolved beyond what I like to call "your exclusive identification with ego" to a lived identity with your Unique Self, your relationship with your wounds will dramatically shift. Your Unique Self lives and breathes aligned with the larger evolutionary framework, and it is seeking to contribute your Unique Gifts for the sake of the larger whole. In such a large context, the evolutionary perspective of Unique Self naturally puts your wounds in perspective.

This means that you will be able to see your wounds from a kosmocentric perspective instead of from an egocentric perspective. Identifying yourself as a Unique expression of the divine, responsible for co-creating the next evolutionary leap toward greater love, inclusion, and embrace—the kosmocentric perspective—obviously places your wounds in such a wider lens that your personal obsession with the insults of your life is exposed for the narcissism that it is.

But narcissism it is—only in part. Holding your enlightened kosmocentric realization more deeply, you understand that you are not merely part of the whole, in the sense of being a cog in a machine or a link in a process. Rather your part is the whole itself.

Your part—that is to say, you—has infinite value, dignity, and worth. *The pain of your part, your pain, is the pain of All-That-Is. God, the love and compassion that is the substantial reality of All-That-Is, feels your pain.* You and God meet in empathetic embrace within the depth of your wounding, for which God cries.

When we talk about the infinite nature of the divine, we refer not only to the infinity of divine power or the infinity of the divine process. We refer also to the infinity of divine pain for the wounds of every finite being. God is not only the infinity of power, but no less the infinity of intimacy. In Kabbalah this is called the pain of the Shechina in exile; in Christianity it came to be called the mystery of incarnation. The momentous insight into the infinite dignity of the individual is a realization of the dignity of the tears of every finite being. This is the great paradox of your wounds. The abuse you suffered infinitely matters. *And from the context of your larger evolutionary Unique Self, you can forgive and move on, held in the fierce embrace of the evolutionary creativity and Unique Gifts that are yours to manifest and give in this lifetime.*

When we move beyond the personal, we are moving not to the impersonal, but to the transpersonal. This is an evolutionary and not a regressive move. In taking a dismissive posture in regard to your wounds because you have begun to identify with the impersonal, this teaching commits a classic pre-trans fallacy. It confuses that which is pre- with that which is trans. For example, this fallacy confuses the pre-personal that appears before the appropriate development of the healthy personal ego and the transpersonal that trance-ends and includes the healthy personal ego. A baby and an enlightened sage may both be said to be "not stuck" in personality. However, the baby is pre-personal (and pre-rational), while the enlightened sage is transpersonal (and transrational). The difference is that while the baby has not yet evolved to the mature individuation of the personal, the enlightened sage has first achieved a mature personal individuation, and only afterward, transcended the personal. But even in that transcendence, the enlightened sage does not exclude the personal, but rather transcends and includes the personal. In a pre-trans fallacy, the pre-personal and impersonal are implicitly lumped together, and then conflated with the transpersonal. That is a colossal mistake. The dignity of the personal is the dignity of your story. *Your Unique Self story is the core of your Eros.* Your story, as we have seen, is not to be confused with the pseudo-Eros and pseudo-story of your ego.

When you move from personal to transpersonal, the core rules for the healthy ascension to higher levels of consciousness always apply. You must always transcend and *include* the previous level. A transrational mysticism must transcend and include the rational—there are places where the merely rational cannot go. However, the transrational must never be confused with the pre-rational, which is superstitious and often antirational. Similarly, the transpersonal must transcend and *include* the personal.

Evolutionary We Space

This understanding of the paradoxical relationship between the transpersonal and the personal, the knowing that the transpersonal must always transcend and include the personal, is precisely the difference between an evolutionary spiritual community and a cult. Enter either one on a Sunday morning, and from the outside, they look strikingly similar. In both, groups of people may be chanting, swaying, meditating, or praying. When you enter the room, you can palpably feel that you are not entering personal but collective space.

To determine whether you are in a cult or an evolutionary We Space, you need to enter the interior face of the group's consciousness. One of the most precise and powerful ways to do so is to check its relationship to the personal.

Has the group transcended and included or has it excluded the personal? It is pretty easy to tell. Decision making and personal autonomy are key litmus tests.

Can you legitimately hold a perspective different from the leader? How easy or hard is it to leave? Is the leader held to be perfect and egoless, and everyone else flawed and trapped in ego? Is clearly abusive behavior that flagrantly violates personal boundaries acceptable under the guise of ego-busting?

We need to be very careful here. It is fully possible for a spiritual community to have a strong leader who has a contract with his or her students to rigorously challenge their egoic attachment. That contract may allow for what has been called "crazy wisdom" behavior that would not be acceptable from your boss at work. The hypersensitive self is rooted not in the Unique Liberated Self, but in the ego. There are profound systems of guru yoga that challenge the egoic predicament. Whether such a system is in fact motivated by the pure intention and integrity of the leader, or has been subtly hijacked by the sophisticated ego of the leader, is next to impossible to ascertain from the outside.

A critical distinction must be drawn between the dignity of the personal and the ego. They are not the same, and the teacher and student must profoundly honor the former even while challenging the latter. The job of the true teacher is to comfort the afflicted and afflict the comfortable.

The Wounds of Love or The Idolatry of Hurt

Evolution beyond exclusive identification with ego, whether through prayer, meditation, or ethical mindfulness, profoundly transforms your relationship to your wounds. The deeper awakening to your Evolutionary Unique Self deepens that transformation in significant ways. Evolutionary awakening beyond exclusive identification with ego is essential to any person who wants to live a decent life. It is for that reason that decade ago I began to write about what I called then, the democratization of enlightenment.[64]

Clearly, in the Western context, there has been an obsessive and even narcissistic emphasis on personal hurt. It is further true that when the ego is the center of gravity of your person, then the ego will experience hurt as a terrible insult to your very existence.

---

64 I coined the term "democratization of enlightenment" many years ago, and it has been a major motif in my teaching. It appeared in print and in the virutal space over the last decade many times before it showed up in an actual book. See *Radical Kabbalah* (2012) and *Your Unique Self* (2012).

There is also a forthcoming ebook by this name: Gafni, M. & Student, S. (2014). *Democratization of enlightenment*. Integral Wisdom Press. Manuscript in preparation.

Your hurt activates the ritual of rejection, and degenerative patterns of recrimination are activated. In order to assert your power, you seek to hurt the one whom you feel hurt you. By damaging the one who hurt you, your ego is sated. You have proven to your hypersensitive, empty self, and to whomever the spectators might be, that you exist and that you are powerful. You have done this in the most degraded way, by inflicting hurt. In the contemporary context of our victim culture, saying "I was hurt" is all too often a justification for the most insidiously motivated malice. "Being hurt" has become a free pass that forgives all malicious and even heinous behavior.

It is only through divine communion in which you access your larger self, that you learn the freedom of staying open as love despite and through the hurt. You practice staying open as love through the pain. You turn the egoic insults to the small self into the wounds of love of the Unique Self. *Expand the context of your consciousness. Widen your circle of caring and concern. The obsession with your wound will begin to dissipate and ultimately disappear as you begin to realize your own liberation.*

Let me tell you a story I first read in a Buddhist text some decades back:

There was a woman—Kiso Gotami may have been her name—who was so broken, to whom life had dealt such a harsh hand, that she simply was unable to get up in the morning. So she went to the Buddha and asked what she could do. She had come to the end. Life was just too painful. The Buddha said to her, "If you bring me a mustard seed from a house that knows no sorrow, then all will be well with you."

She thought, "This will be very simple." Life was hard for her, but so many of her neighbors led such easy, happy lives.

She knocked on the door of her neighbor's house, the couple with the wonderful relationship and seven smiling children. She told them, "The Buddha has told me to bring a mustard seed from a house that knows no sorrow, and all will be well with me. I know you have such a joyous house! Might you please spare me a mustard seed?"

They looked at her almost angrily and said, "You have no idea what is going on in our house. You don't know about . . . " and they began to tell her of the tragedies they had suffered—a tale of secret woe and hidden sorrow the likes of which she had never heard.

We think we know so well what is going on in someone else's reality.

She hears their story. She decides to stay for a short time and offer comfort. A good while later, she leaves and goes to the next house. She is sure this house is a house of joy with no sorrow. She asks again for a mustard seed. The response is again, "Why did you come to us? You think we're a house with no sorrow?" They begin to tell her their story of sadness and woe.

What can she do? Again, she is so moved, she wants to comfort them. She stays with the second family for a period of time, comforting, soothing, and trying to cheer them.

She goes to a third house and again meets the same story of sorrow. Her compassion is aroused once again. She stays with them and comforts them as well.

So it continues from house to house. She is comforted as she comforts. Her ego falls away as she enters the Unique calling of her life and realizes her liberation.

When you add an alignment with the evolutionary impulse itself to this teaching of compassion, the obsession with wounds begins to take on a sense of the ridiculous. By widening or deepening your context hurt takes on its right proportion. This is good.

Lying About Your Hurt to Support Your Ego

You need to engage in a true reality consideration to consider how much you have actually been hurt. Is your ego hurt or is your Unique Self hurt? What advantages are you receiving from your hurt? How are you manipulating and even lying about your hurt to prop up your otherwise contracted identity?

It is critical for you to remember that hurt is a "state." All states, whether they be altered, drunken, mystical, or sexual states, are temporary.

The state overtakes you and shifts your consciousness. Then, however, you invariably return to what for you is your more natural state of consciousness. At that point, you begin, without even being aware that you are doing it, to interpret your state experience. All states of being are subject to interpretation through many different prisms—cultural, social, psychological, emotional, and developmental. For example, developmentally, states are interpreted through the prism of the stage of consciousness in which the person experiencing the state usually locates.[65]

A stage, unlike a state, is not passing and temporary. It is rather a stable and irreversible level of consciousness. In every line of development, there are clearly discernible stages. For example, in motor development, there is a stage before and a stage after a child is able to ride a bike. In cognitive development, there is a before-reading stage and an after-reading stage. In mathematical development, there is a significant cognitive leap after the multiplication tables. And in moral development, there are four distinct stages that have been identified as egocentric, ethnocentric, worldcentric, and kosmocentric. Each level is based on who is in your circle of felt caring and concern.

States do not yield any information by themselves, but are always interpreted through the prism of stages. It is for this reason that so many aphorisms suggest that a person's true level of consciousness and interior psychological self is revealed when they are drunk. Some people get very kind and open when drunk, and others, surprisingly, seem to get very mean and cruel. Some reveal their open heart, and others reveal their racism. Their ethnocentric stage of consciousness is revealed by the drink.

Mystical states are also interpreted through the prism of stages of consciousness.

Let's say you have a genuine mystical experience. If you are at an egocentric level of moral development, you will interpret it to mean that you are enlightened. If you are obsessively egocentric in a highly narcissistic way, you may think that you are the only enlightened being on the planet.

---

65 See K. Wilber (2006). *Integral spirituality*, Boston: Shambhala.

If you have the same experience, and you are at an ethnocentric level of consciousness, then you may well believe that your people and no others are the chosen people of God. If you are at a worldcentric level of consciousness, you will be more likely to interpret your experience as a call that obligates you to engage in healing and transformation on a global scale.

If you are at a kosmocentric stage of consciousness, then the level of depth and wisdom with which you approach the global activism sparked by your mystical state will be of a fundamentally deeper quality. Kosmocentric implies an expansive and integral embrace of all systems and forms of knowing available to you. So, for example, from a kosmocentric level of consciousness, you bring to the situation you are engaging an integrated mind, body, and heart, and a whole-systems understanding of the evolutionary possibilities available to meet the moment. Your wisdom merges profound reverence for the past, penetrating insight into the present, and a humble boldness toward the future. Your state, in this case a mystical state, is always interpreted through your level of consciousness.

Hurt is a state. This is a huge insight. You need to really take it in. Hurt is not an objective reality that gives you license for cruelty under the cover of "I was hurt." *Hurt is a state, and it is interpreted through your stage or level of consciousness. As you evolve, your relationship to your wounds naturally shifts. More than any other single barometer, what you do with your hurt reveals to you and others your genuine level of consciousness.* When you feel hurt, the masks of piety and the guises of liberation from ego are stripped away, and your naked heart is revealed to yourself and those with eyes to see.

Once you approach your hurt from this wider context, you can begin to appreciate the next instruction. Here it is in the form of a story:

The Hasidic master Naftali of Rophsitz told his students a tale of great healers being called to help the king. The king's son was crying desperately. All the wise men of the kingdom, the doctors, the magicians, and shamans (the psychologists of the day) had been to see him, and none could comfort him or stop his crying. Indeed, every attempt at healing seemed to intensify the young prince's woe.

It happened that an old woman from the hinterland of the kingdom was bringing milk to the palace. She passed the boy as he wandered, sobbing, near the kitchen. She approached him, not realizing he was the king's son, and whispered a few words in his ear.

Lo and behold, he looked up at her, and his crying began to abate. In just a few minutes, he was not crying at all. And here Naftali ended his tale.

"Please, holy master," the disciples pleaded with their teacher, "you must tell us. What magic, what amulet, what secret did the old wise woman—who we know must have been the Shekhinah herself—what did she say?" The master smiled. "It was very simple," he said. "She told the boy, 'You must not cry more than it hurts.'"

If we learn to live wide open even as we are hurt by love, then the divine wakes up to its own True Nature. *To be firm in your knowing of love, even when you are desperate, and to be strong in your heart of forgiveness even when you are betrayed, this is what it means to be holy.*

Hurt is a state. You must always ask what has been hurt—your Unique Self or your ego. Then you must ask how much have you genuinely been hurt and what license your hurt does or does not give you. People lost in victimhood, making exaggerated or false claims, often inflict a thousandfold more hurt on their alleged abuser than the actual or imagined hurt they are claiming. We must always protect the abused. We need, however, to be very discerning, for sometimes the abusers disguise themselves as the abused. Lost in the egoic hypersensitive self, the true abusers have failed to align themselves with the larger context of the evolutionary impulse. When you do align yourself with your evolutionary obligation, your Unique Self, you do not ignore your wounds; however, your *attachment* to your wounds falls to the wayside.

You can let go of your own hurt as you embrace the wider evolutionary context. But you dare not do so with the hurt of another. *Yes, you can and must demand that they not cry more than it hurts. You can and must demand that they not hurt others from the place of their untransformed wound. If they move to inflict hurt in such ways, you must hold them accountable before the bar of integrity and justice. This is absolutely true even if the impulse that moved them to maliciously inflict hurt was the confusion and pain of their own sense of woundedness. All the more so when the objective hurt they inflict exponentially exceeds the subjective and relatively minor wounds they received.*

And yet, after all these caveats, and after we align with the larger evolutionary impulse that is beyond the personal—we need to never lose the full intensity of compassion for all personal suffering. Even when it is self-inflicted, narcissistic, and unnecessary. To judge which suffering will receive our love and compassion is a tricky business, with multiple egoic traps along the way.

The liberated prophet Isaiah channels the following divine teaching: *bekol tzaratam lo tzar.* "In all of your pain, God is in pain." This refers not only to legitimate pain. Even petty and self-inflicted pain is felt and held by God.

The Hebrew word *tzar* means both pain and contraction. For the prophetic teaching refers not only to necessary pain. It refers rather to the majority of our pain, which is unnecessary and even frivolous. All of this pain is at its root a result of self-contraction. The prophetic channeling of the divine voice by Isaiah can be literally translated from the Hebrew as "In all of your contraction, God is contracted."

The way to open your heart through the pain is to find the God that is infinitely pained in your contraction. It is that God which leads from the narrow constriction of your pain to walk again in the wide spaces of your heart.

When the ego's heart breaks, then the heart closes and contracts.

When the Unique Self's heart breaks, the heart opens through the pain into greater love.

The divine is dependent on us. In the direct language of the Unique Self Kabbalists, "Your actions either weaken or empower God." When you expand, the divine surges with power and ecstasy, and expands with you and as you. When you recoil into your small, petty, egoic self, the divine contracts with you and as you. But in that contraction, God also feels your pain. We may live lives of quiet desperation, but there are truly no lives of lonely desperation, for God is always with us in our pain.

You are invited to *imitatio dei,* the "imitation of the divine." Imitate no one except God. Just as God never forsakes the personal for the sake of the process, so too never let go of your empathy and compassion, even for self-inflicted suffering.

The prophets never close their hearts. When someone hurts, they say, "Oh my God, you hurt so badly! Let me hold you and love you. I know you may have done to this yourself, and I will hold you accountable for it tomorrow. But at this very moment, I do not care. I just want to hold you and make it better."

Facing Through the Fear of Death

The movement taught by all the great teachers from ego to True Self is referred to by some as the hero's journey.

It is called *ratzo* by the great enlightened prophet Ezekiel. *Ratzo* means "to run" or "to desire." *Ratzo* is the ecstatic running toward God, who is the spacious Ground of Being.

At that precise point of realization, however, when you have fallen into the spaciousness of True Self, you are required to do what Ezekiel calls *shov.*

You turn. You turn back and face life fully without flinching. You are filled with the courage and freedom born in you from your hero's journey.

You feel your Unique Self arising from the ashes of your ego. You feel the full power and humility of your Unique Self coursing through you. *You have transformed your fate as ego into your destiny as a Unique Self. Every detour in your life has revealed itself to be a necessary destination on the way to your destiny.* You are now ready to begin your second hero's journey as a Unique Self living passionately and fully in deep and joyful service to God and your fellow beings. When you awaken to this realization, the fear of death—which was only the fear of not having responded to the Unique Obligation of your life—disappears.

You may wake up early in life or later. *At any point in which you are moved to respond to your evolutionary obligation, you can heal the past. You can heal the past with sincere right action or sincere right intention. There is no such thing as being too late. The potential for radical awakening and change is present at every moment.* You are then radically shocked and wildly ecstatic when you realize the complete and total identity between your purpose and God's purpose. This is the true meaning of evolutionary alignment with the ecstatic God-impulse that lives in you and calls you to service.

More Than Personal, Not Less Than Personal

Your ability to choose your own evolution is the God-impulse in you. The mystery of your free choice, in defiance of every force of inertia and downward gravitational pull exerted by all the painful and traumatic circumstances of your life, is the mystery of God pulsating in you, as you, and through you. That does not mean, as some evolutionary-spirituality teachers mistakenly suggest, that there is no God *beyond* you. Of course there is. It would be a rather grand narcissism to think that you alone exhaust all of divinity.

This incarnation of God in You is not the limit of God. It is but one face of the divine, the first person of God. God discloses in the second person as well. Just look at the Unique Self of your friend. And in third person, just look at the wonders of nature.

It also does not mean that God is merely process and principle. The divine is also infinitely personal. This is the infinity of intimacy that lies at the heart of the kosmos. To say God is not personal is much the same as to say that God is not physical.

I once read a spiritually tragic report of Jewish schoolchildren who were asked to draw God. The papers came back either entirely empty or with pallid drawings, empty of life. The children had been raised on the classic sacred teaching of the nonphysicality of God. But the teaching has not been transmitted properly. When we say that God is not physical, we mean to say that God is *more* than physical, not less. We mean to say that the infinite depth of God's realness cannot be exhausted or even approximated by the shallow reality of the physical. It is much the same when we say that God is not personal.

When we say that God is not personal, we mean that the quality of personal that is God is not limited to a particular person. In the language of the Zohar, "There is no place devoid of God." Second, we mean that the personal as we know it cannot begin to exhaust the infinite personal intimacy, caring, and love that is the divine. God is not personal in a human-personality sense. But this is because the limited personal quality of the separate self cannot hold the infinite reality or the infinite tenderness of God's loving embrace.

Yearn for the beloved in whose bosom you may rest and before whom you are privileged to chant in radical devotion and insane joy. Prostrate yourself wonderstruck before the love intelligence that expresses itself as All-That-Is. In all of these, you will feel the God that is both within you and beyond you. Know that where you fall, you fall into the infinitely personal divine embrace. God is process, principle, and personal plus.

It would be a horrific loss to lose our devotion. It would be a violation of deeper truth to lose our ability to bow before God as Thou. It would inflict a great wound in God if we lost our yearning for the beloved God. To lose our passionate attachment to God as second person under the guise of an impersonal evolutionary spirituality or an impersonal Buddhist teaching is to lose our belongingness in the world. When teachers of evolutionary spirituality proclaim, "No one else can save us. There is no God beyond that. Never was, is, not now, and never will be," they are telling only half the story. It is a partial truth. When it is made into a whole, it is distorting, damaging, and destructive. It undermines our ability to evolve and realize higher levels of truth and consciousness. Nikos Kazantzakis was right. We are the saviors of God. We are responsible for the evolution of God. But that gift was given to us by God in love.

The God who gave us that gift is always catching us when we fall. Again and again, wherever we fall, we fall into God's arms. We live in the arms of the beloved. Process, principle, and personal God are all different faces of the One. The divinely evolved ability to hold paradox in our very body and being is the necessary faculty of awakened consciousness.

It All Depends on You Personally

The experience of being personally implicated in the evolution of All-That-Is is central to evolutionary mystical consciousness. Every right act done by a human being was understood by the evolutionary mystics as effecting a *tikkun,* an evolutionary fixing of the kosmos. One of the many formulas deployed by the evolutionary mystics was *leshem yichud,* "This act is for the sake of the unification/evolution of consciousness." This interior realization of awakened consciousness is captured in the simple biblical words "God spoke to Abraham."

God actually spoke to every individual Being, but it was Abraham who *heard.* God did not choose Abraham. Abraham chose God. *To live awake in an evolutionary context is to be personally addressed.* The evolutionary mystics of Kabbalah unveil the esoteric reading of the wisdom maxim: "Know that which is above you," taught by the old wise masters of the second and third centuries. In the evolutionary mystical reading, this maxim is understood to say, "Know that which is above you Depends On You!"

DISTINCTION TEN: THE NATURAL VS. THE DOGMATIC NATURE OF FREE CHOICE

The place where the personal re-insinuates itself in Authentic Self teaching, but without being named as such, is in the issue of choice. The discussion of choice is the final critical distinction between Unique Self and Authentic Self teaching. For Unique Self, which holds a dialectic between the personal and the impersonal, a similar dialectic exists between choice and choicelessness. For Authentic Self, which radically rejects the personal, but dogmatically embraces choice, the fine dialectic between choice and choicelessness is lost and with it the implicit compassion and ability to hold complexity that comes from that distinction. I will unfold this distinction in greater depth in a fuller essay on this topic, but for now let me just paint in broad brushstrokes the apparent contradiction in regard to the place of the personal, inherent in the discussion of choice in the Authentic Self model. The source of the personal is the personal free-functioning will that initiated the cosmos. This is an essential realization that needs to be deeply considered. The revelation of the personal takes place at the precise moment when the un-manifest decides to manifest. In that moment of the Great Flaring Forth, popularly known as the big bang and theistically referred to as Creation, the personal face of essence is disclosed. Borrowing from Buddhist metaphor, we might say that original face decides to become Unique face, or drawing from Whitehead, we might say that Being discloses the face of Becoming. The free nature of the cosmos discloses its intensely personal nature. The universe is intelligent, and that intelligence in its personal, non-dual quality "decides" to initiate the kosmos as we know it. Both Authentic Self teachings and Unique Self teaching prioritize the centrality of this notion of free will and choice, which harkens back to the initiating moment when nothing decided to become something.

However, in the Authentic Self teaching, the connections between these factors, the personal and free quality of the cosmos, the free will of the individual, and the quality of the personal as an expression of enlightenment, seems to have been overlooked. So strangely, Authentic Self teaching dogmatically denies the essential quality of the personal in the individual, and equally assertively, insists on the absolute free will of the individual. But, if there is no individual beyond "bundles of impulses," and the level beyond the personal is the impersonal process, where does free will come from? Unique Self teaching absolutely affirms free will as an expression of personal essence, which is identical with the personal essence that decided that nothing should be something. For Unique Self, it is precisely the individuated quality of the personal beyond ego, which is the matrix of free will beyond ego. However, for Authentic Self teaching, which denies the essential quality of the individuated personal, it is difficult to interpret the source and nature of free will. *Evolutionary Enlightenment* says:

"It takes courage and humility to let in how much of what you consider to be uniquely you has actually been shaped by the evolutionary process and the world around you" (p. 151).

In the immediately following passage, the book goes on to enumerate a long list of factors shaping the emergence of the personal self. "As you see through the illusion of the personal, you will recognize the truth that who we are as human beings is a bundle of impulses, reactions, and habits, conditioned patterns that together create the convincing appearance of unique individuality" (p. 149). The point being made is that your personal self is an illusion, which is actually shaped by a vast array of impersonal forces.

Paradoxically, however, on the issue of choice, Authentic Self *inconsistently* makes the opposite argument. The same list of conditional factors given for human beings as "a bundle of impulses, reactions, and habits, conditioned patterns that together create the convincing appearance of unique individuality" (p. 149) that are said to warrant denying the ontology of the personal are also listed as potential reasons to deny the ontology of free will.

Nonetheless, free will is asserted even in the face of the identical factors that were used to deny the personal. Now, to be clear, Unique Self also affirms free will. However, Unique Self teaching roots choice in the quality of the personal, which in the realization of the Unique Self enlightenment, is the innermost face of essence. Or, at the very least, it is a paradoxical face of the impersonal that lives in dialectical union with the impersonal. But it makes little sense to say, on the one hand, that the impersonal developmental process negates the existence of the personal, but does not negate freedom of choice.

In fact, the passages in the Authentic Self teaching which affirm choice—which I fully agree with—all sound suspiciously personal:

"Just imagine—without free agency, who would you be? Little more than a robot, unconsciously responding and reacting to conditioned egoic fears and desires, cultural triggers, biological impulses, and external stimuli, with no control over your own destiny" (p. 69).

Of course, this same list of conditioned factors was used in *Evolutionary Enlightenment* to dismiss the personal. But, if the personal self is an illusion, then who is choosing?

"If there is a measure of freedom, then there *is* freedom to choose. And it is very important to understand that this choosing faculty alone is what makes conscious evolution possible" (p. 70).

Choice is "not easy" because "[T]he human self is by nature a complex multidimensional process, and within that process are many factors that limit our freedom and obscure our awareness.... There are layers of cultural conditioning, values and assumptions about how things *should* be that color our perspectives without us even knowing it.... *All of this is you.* And yet it *is* possible to take responsibility for all of these dimensions of who you are, through the transformative recognition that *you are always the one who is choosing*" (p. 71, emphasis in original).

I completely agree with this citation. The Unique Self, which is the personal face of the process, is always choosing. In Authentic Self teachings, however, *you* always refers to the "impersonal evolutionary impulse" (70). You are the one making the choice. After all, who could it be?

"*And you, whoever you are, are always choosing*" (p. 70, emphasis in original).

"That is why, when you are trying to evolve at the level of consciousness, you have to deal with an enormous number of biological, emotional, psychological, and culturally inherited habits" (p. 72).

"Enormous effort, will-power, and intention will be required, especially at the beginning of the path, to break through these accumulated habits at all levels of your being" (p. 71).

"If you aspire to evolve, if you intend to become a conscious vehicle for the evolutionary impulse, you have to use the God-given powers of awareness and conscious choice to navigate between your new and higher spiritual aspirations, and all of the conditioned impulses and habits that are embedded in your self-system" (p. 73).

Authentic Self presents choice in a way that is not dissimilar to my assertion of Uniqueness, with one major distinction: uniqueness is *prima facie* self evident, empirically verifiable from a developmental perspective, and accessible through realization. Simply stated, "self-evident" means that there is no appearance in the world, which is not unique. And, once we understand the great insight of the Buddhist teacher Nagarjuna that there is no arising of form without consciousness and no spirit or consciousness without form, we begin to realize that uniqueness, which on human levels is an expression of the personal, is undeniable. In relation to choice, which is necessary for an empowered human being, the Authentic Self teachings are willing to make the leap and to hold the paradox of determinism and freedom, but Authentic Self teaching is unwilling to hold paradox in the relation between impersonal and personal or between uniqueness and oneness.

CHAPTER 4:
BETWEEN EGO AND UNIQUE SELF

The primary critique of Unique Self teaching, leveled by students of Authentic Self in all of its names—for example, evolutionary self—is that Unique Self is but a clever front for ego. Or that even if it is not actually identical with ego, it can all to easily be hijacked by the ego. The latter is a fair and important point. However, the same critique might be just as easily leveled at the clarion call to identity with the evolutionary impulse that lies at the heart of both Unique and Authentic Self teachings. (The difference, as we have already noted, is that in the Authentic Self teaching, the evolutionary impulse is wholly impersonal, while in the Unique Self teaching, the evolutionary impulse at its core is expressed only personally through you as the personal face of the process). It is all too easy for the ego to hijack the evolutionary impulse as a fig leaf for every manner of ego's misdeed. Indeed, this is not a theoretical concern, but a sadly well proved truth as the history of the evolutionary movements show. The grandchildren of Hegel's evolutionary teaching, communism primary among them, deployed the evolutionary imperative to cover every form of heinous crime against humanity. And yet, that does not invalidate the sacred power of the evolutionary impulse, just as the crimes committed in the name of Christ do not deconstruct the truth and beauty of Christ consciousness, nor does the atom bomb disqualify the nobility of the humanist creative urge born of the new scientific paradigm. Nor does the fact that ego might hijack Unique Self lessen the critical nature of Unique Self realization. All goods may be hijacked. We must, therefore, guard against the hijacking, but we must not refuse to fly. To guard against the conflation of ego and Unique Self, it is necessary to clearly discern between these two very different states and stages of consciousness. Below, I offer the beginning of a discussion of just such a set of discernments. My students, friends, and colleagues Heather Fester and Kerstin Tuschik have elaborated on these distinctions in a wonderful ebook.[66] But for now, allow me to offer this first set of twenty-six distinctions between ego and Unique Self.

Twenty-Six Distinctions between Ego and Unique Self

As I have already pointed out above, ego and Unique Self are two very different stages and states of consciousness. At the level of ego, you must let go of the illusion of specialness. At the level of Unique Self, you must embrace the infinite gorgeousness of your specialness and the obligation that it creates for you to give your deepest Unique Gifts in the world.

Unique Self, which is your Unique Perspective, creates your Unique Gifts, which in turn creates your Unique Obligation to offer your gift.

This entire linked set of unfolding realizations is predicated on the discernment between Unique Self and ego. This discernment is

---

66 Tuschik, K. & Fester, H. (2014). Distinctions between ego and Unique Self: Elaboration on the original distinctions by Marc Gafni in *Your Unique Self: The radical path to personal enlightenment* with practices. Ebook. Center for Integral Wisdom Press.

essential to prevent ego from hijacking Unique Self. So what we need to do at this point is deepen our grasp of that discernment, which is all-important for the realization of your Unique Self enlightenment.

To live a successful life of realization, power, and genuine attainment, you must be able to discern—in real time—between expressions of your separate self or ego and your Unique Self. In the following section, I will draw a number of distinctions between Unique Self (station five) and ego, which I refer to in the eight stations as separate self (station two). The purpose of these distinctions is to serve as pointing-out instructions that will help you make the discernment between ego and Unique Self in your own first-person experience.

The ego and Unique Self dualities that I offer below are—like all dualities—not ultimate.

Reality is more intimate than ultimate. Reality is ultimately and intimately non-dual and thus far more fluid and complex than this set of dualities.

Nevertheless, to develop into your enlightenment, you must begin with essential discernments between these different qualities of ego and Unique Self. The ability to spontaneously access these discernments is an essential step toward your Unique Self enlightenment.

1) Separate or Part of the Whole

The most elemental distinction between Unique Self and ego is that ego is a state of separateness. Ego is apart and not part of the larger whole. Unique Self emerges from a larger wholeness. It is unique but not separate, a distinct expression of the one. For this reason Unique does not come fully online until and unless one has had at least a glimmer or taste of either the—classical, first person True Self enlightenment—or, of being called to service while being held in the embrace of the second-person God. In Buddhist terms, one might say that Unique Self comes online after a taste of emptiness or sunyata. In Christian terms, one might say that Unique Self comes online after meeting Christ. In the dialectical paradox of first-person and second-person realizations, you show up as Christ after you have met Christ. In Jewish terms, you realize Unique Self after the encounter. The encounter begins with the first tasting of the commanding presence of the ethical god who both holds you and lives in you as your soul. Or from a mystical perspective, from the presence that also lives in and as your Self. It is important to emphasize that you do not need a full realization of True Self or the encounter to begin to realize Unique Self. And it is naturally the case that the deeper and more stable your realization of True Self or the encounter, the deeper and more steady is your realization of Unique Self.

2) Special or Not Special

Your ego thinks that you are special because you are better or worse than other people. Your Unique Self knows you are special because you are yourself. For the ego, "special" means "better than." For your Unique Self, "special" or "different" means distinct and free from any comparison or point of reference. Your specialness is your spontaneous experience of your essence.

3) Action or Reaction

Ego reacts. Unique Self acts. Your ego is constantly in reaction to outside stimuli. It never thinks a spontaneous thought. It rarely acts because it is moved to do so by a freely arising thought or desire. Unique Self is moved to action by the power and joy of its own authentic original impulse.

4) Imitation or Originality

Ego imitates. Unique Self is original. Your ego is trapped in imitation. For the ego is, by its very definition, in limitation. Limitation leads to imitation. So the ego is always living the life of limitation based on imitation, which leads to mindless competition. Your ego is in constant competition, which leads to compulsive comparison and dissatisfaction. Originality, which is a quality of Unique Self, freed from the tyranny of comparison, is by its nature both urgently creative and self-satisfied.

Your ego never thinks an original thought. Originality emerges from your Unique Face, which is evoked by contact with your Original Face. "Original Face" is the Buddhist way of describing the experience of sustained contact with the eternal, transcendent Ground of Being. Originality gives birth to action beyond reaction. Your Unique Becoming emerges from your immersion in Being.

5) Satisfaction or Greed

Your separate self is driven by greed. Greed is not the want of anything specific. Rather, it is insatiable want that creates perpetual anxiety. Insatiable want is a structure of the egoic mind, which seeks more and more identity enhancers to confirm its existence. Satisfaction and ego are opposites.

Give the ego everything, and it will not be satisfied. Give the Unique Self anything, and it will be grateful and satisfied. Satisfied, not resigned. Satisfaction emerges from the fullness of whatever the moment brings. Satisfaction comes from contact with Being and from doing your radical, intense best in the world of Becoming without attachment to outcome.

Being is all one, so any moment of Authentic Being gives infinite satisfaction. Becoming is an expression of the evolutionary impulse and not merely of the egoic drive to achieve. So for Unique Self, your very best is always good enough. For your ego, your very best is never good enough.

This is why the ego is the source of all your suffering. It always wants more to fill its greed.

Greed, however, is not a root evil. At its core, greed is your ego's distortion of a quality of essence, the quality of pure infinite desire. Infinite desire is the natural expression of the endless creativity of essence. It is this quality that creates constant yearning, especially the yearning to grow, to create. This yearning, however, lives in paradoxical harmony with satisfaction.

6) Enough or More

Your ego thinks that there is never enough to go around. It always needs more to feel like it exists at all. Your Unique Self knows that it is enough. Your Unique Self knows that there is enough to go around. *Your Unique Self strives for more, not to fill the emptiness but as an expression of the fullness of its being—bursting forth as the evolutionary impulse of the kosmos.*

7) Ego Story or Unique Self Story

Enlightenment requires your ability to discern between your ego story and your Unique Self story. Your separate-self egoic personality has needs. It wants to make itself feel secure. So your ego tells you a story about yourself that makes you feel safe, valuable, and worthy. The inability to feel safe, valuable, and worthy is a devastating experience for the ego, one it will ward off at virtually all costs. So the ego hijacks everything that happens to you, and everything that you do, into a story about its own goodness, value, and worth.

The ego has a simple if ingenious mechanism for doing this. It disguises its ambition, its drive for power, or its insecure grasping, and converts them into narrative material that supports its own positive self-image. This is how the separate-self ego story develops. It is this story that teachers of True Self correctly tell you to leave behind when they say, "To be enlightened you must let go of your story."

One of the places in which you can see with naked clarity the mechanisms deployed by the ego to disguise its primal needs and present them as a "good story" is your dream life. To move beyond the ego's story, you must be able to look at the story from the outside. You must wake up and identify the true root cause of your experience in the dream that has been disguised by the ego as *story*. One simple example, which highlights the hidden dynamics of the ego's deceptive narrative, occurs when you awaken from a dream and you realize that its elaborate story, which climaxes in you urinating, is really the ego's story. The literary ego weaves a narrative tapestry when really what is happening is that you just need to urinate. That is a great relief and a great realization.

This is an essential part of the process of enlightenment or awakening. What you are essentially doing is dis-identifying with your story or perspective, and then taking a perspective on your perspective.[67] You are letting your story become an object, so that you can see it and understand the root motivations and dynamics that are really at play in your story. When that happens, there is space for your more authentic story to arise, which reflects not the grasping of the separate-self ego but the utterly resplendent uniqueness of your Unique Self. This is your Unique Self story.

8) Joy or Fear

The Unique Self is in joy. Joy is the natural by-product of living your Unique Self story. The ego is rarely happy and often plagued by an underlying feeling of fear, deadness, or depression. The happiness that the ego does experience is of a heavier and less richly textured quality than the joy of the Unique Self. The joy of the Unique Self is lighter and freer, often verging on the ecstatic.

9) Open Heart or Closed Heart

When the ego's heart breaks, then the heart closes and contracts. *When the Unique Self's heart breaks, the heart opens through the pain into greater love.* For your ego, the interior face of the kosmos is at best a concept. For Unique Self, the interior face of the kosmos is the infinity of intimacy.

10) Eros or Grasping

The ego is not erotic. Unique Self lives in Eros. To live in Eros means to live with fullness of presence and with a felt sense of wholeness. It is to yearn urgently and ecstatically, without grasping and to experience interiority, the feeling of being on the inside. This is the experience of Unique Self. The ego lives with the feeling of always being on the outside. It fragments, grasps, and never shows up fully present to other. Unique Self lives in Eros.

11) Authentic Freedom or Pseudofreedom

Your ego is a slave that wants to be free. Freedom is the quality that we call autonomy. Your ego, however, understands and experiences freedom/autonomy as freedom from external influence. Only then does ego feel free to do what it wants. *Unique Self is free. Unique*

---

67   See A. H. Almaas, *The Pearl Beyond Price* (Boston: Shambhala, 2001).

Self understands and experiences freedom as the freedom to live your Uniqueness and give your deepest gifts in the world.

When you feel yourself demanding your egoic freedom, stop for a moment and feel into it. Do not cover over the emptiness that lies at the root of your desire for freedom and autonomy. Feel into the emptiness. Feel into the hole. For example: Perhaps you are in a relationship that you want to leave. You are chafing to get out of the relationship. But as you contemplate this, stay in the discomfort that you can palpably feel—which lies at the root of this desire. For now, do not give the feeling words. Instead, feel the quality of the vacuity and emptiness that arouses the desire. If you stay in it long enough, the emptiness will begin to fill up with being and presence, with your Unique Being and Presence. What happened?

You have discovered that the root of your desire to be free from another was your disconnection from your own personal essence, your Unique Self.

When your Unique Self filled the hole, the desperate desire you felt to leave the group—or the marriage or the job—faded away. That does not mean that you should necessarily stay in the marriage or the job. It does, however, mean that you will make the decision from a grounded place of full presence as your Unique Self, and are therefore far more likely to make the right decision.

12) King or Servant

Ego is the servant pretending to be a king. You are avoiding stepping into your Unique Self for fear of being a king. Your ego thinks it is God, but does not really believe it, so your ego insanely tries to make itself the God it knows it is not. *Your Unique Self knows it is God, so it acts in the world with majesty, audacity, and grace.*

13) Victim or Player

In your ego, you cling to every petty detail of your story. You never let go of any of your wounds. Your mantra is "I hurt; therefore, I am." Therefore, your ego can never wholeheartedly forgive. If it does, the ego's forgiveness is a tactic, not a sacrament. Your Unique Self forgives freely without giving up your own truth.

From the evolutionary context of your Unique Self, you realize that you have a Unique Gift to give to All-That-Is. You are animated, driven, and drawn by that larger vision and obligation. This allows you to place your wounds in a larger perspective. *Your Unique Self is not a victim. It is an audacious player in the Great Story of the evolution of consciousness.*

This larger perspective allows you to begin to let go of the story of your wounds. As it is replaced by the greater story of your Unique Self, delight and obligation begin to emerge.

From the place of your Unique Self, you are able to intuitively balance your outrage at injustice with an intuition about when to give up being right and move on. Because you are able to give up being right without giving up your core identity, it becomes infinitely easier to forgive.

14) Betrayal or Loyalty

The ego betrays. The Unique Self is loyal. When you are in your ego, and things go bad, you are willing—in your fear—to betray virtually anyone. Your ego is easily identifiable by the shallowness of its integrity. If you live in Unique Self and things go bad, you find your way, through thick or thin, to a deeper center of spirit.

15) Authentic Friendship or Pseudofriendship

When you are in ego, you might help friends who are successful and even friends who are down, as long as it does not threaten your position. But you are not capable of truly delighting in your deepest heart in a friend's large success.

When you are in Unique Self, your deepest heart delights in your friend's success, even if there is nothing in it for you at all.

16) Bigger or Smaller

When you are in ego, people feel smaller when you walk into the room. They feel invisible before you. The result is that they feel depleted and in danger. *When you are in your Unique Self, people feel bigger when you walk into the room.* They feel seen by you. They feel your desire to love and give to them.

17) Yes or No

Your ego is always contracting and saying, "No." Even when your ego says, "Yes," it is only because it is afraid to say "No." *Your Unique Self is always expanding and saying "Yes."* Even when you say "No," it is only to make room for a more authentic "Yes."

18) Justice or Injustice

The ego is angry at what is done to it. It very rarely feels the same outrage at what is done to someone else. The Unique Self is not merely outraged against injustice done to its own person; it is hurt and outraged by any and all injustice. The ego often fights large causes of injustice as a way to bolster its grandiosity. *Unique Self fights the battles of injustice in its own backyard, even when there is potential collateral damage to its own power and status.*

19) Responsibility or Excuse

The ego very rarely takes substantive responsibility. When the ego attempts to take responsibility, it creates a painful, virtually unbearable contraction in the self. So the ego becomes the master of the excuse. *The Unique Self is able to take responsibility spontaneously, lightly, and with full gravitas.* The Unique Self holds with equal measure of gravitas and ease its own responsibility and its rightful anger at injustice. Usually, the ego advises the other person to "take responsibility," while the ego itself wallows in the real and imagined offenses that it has suffered.

20) Paradox or Splitting

The ego is always splitting. It always sees dualities, and it cannot hold paradox or complexity. For the ego, others are either enemies or friends. Actions are either good or bad. The separate-self ego has a very hard time stably holding perspectives other than its own for extended periods of time. The Unique Self can naturally hold paradox. Contact with the transcendent within the large field of divine reality allows for the holding of opposites. *Sacred outrage and equanimity live in paradoxical harmony within the Unique Self.*

21) Past or Present

The ego lives in the past, thinking it is the present. Therefore, the ego unconsciously confuses past with present. The ego is unable to create intimacy, which means meeting each other in the fullness of the present moment. To make real contact, you must be personal and present. Only the Unique Self can make contact. *For the Unique Self, the present moment consciously includes the past and anticipates the future.*

The ego confuses the past and the present. When you are confused—thinking you are present in the present while you are actually lost in a past trance—you are unable to act effectively, lovingly, or powerfully in the situation that you are in. And the past remains always unhealed. Several years ago a friend and board member of my organization called me, angry at not being included in a particular email loop. Her anger was full of intensity and flaming aggression, which was vastly disproportionate to the ostensible exclusion from the email loop. I considered asking her to resign from the board, as this was not the first time such an overreaction had occurred. Of course, what was coming up was not her present exclusion, but a very old sense of being excluded. She held this sense of being left out from her early childhood as a girl with four brothers who were better loved by their father.

This inability to discern the past from the present has made her unable to effectively navigate her professional or personal world, because she is always prone to dramatic overreactions that undermine many key relationships. The Unique Self does not confuse the past with the present. When the past comes up in the present, the Unique Self recognizes it for what it is: the past coming up in the present.

The Unique Self then uses the present moment to heal the past. The Unique Self recognizes that the patterns of the past have no true foothold or power in the present.

22) Special Relationship or Open as Love

Your ego always seeks the "special relationship"—in the egoic sense—to cover the pain of your emptiness, and thinks the "special relationship" is better than all the rest of your relationships. The Unique Self does not limit love to one person, even though the traditional definition of marriage or a committed relationship can limit you to one partner at a time. *The Unique Self lives open as love in the world.*

23) Love or Fear

The isolated ego is the root cause of murder, war, and virtually all human suffering. The ego feels its own fragility, its limits, and its ultimate powerlessness. As a result, the ego grasps for ways to assert power and experience aliveness. This causes the acting out of all forms of shadow. When you deconstruct your mistaken identity with the separate-self ego, and instead identify with your distinct path in the seamless quilt of the Uni-verse, the fear dissipates and the love returns. When the contraction of ego uncoils, your Unique Self experiences all of the good—personal love, responsibility, compassion, ethical action, activism, and all the rest—that you previously thought was accessible only through your assertion of a separate self.

The choice between personal love and immersion in True Self is a false choice. There is no contradiction between them whatsoever: The West—motivated by love and the desire to end suffering—affirmed the separate self because it thought this was the only way a person could gain the goods of the encounter, namely personal love, responsibility, contact, intimacy, accountability, compassion, and care. This was a mistake; all of those goods may be realized through the encounter between two Unique Selves who are not separate from each other, but consciously part of the same seamless coat of the Uni-verse. *Personal love does not require two separate selves.*

24) Eternity or Death

The ego strives for immortality it can never achieve, and therefore, displaces its grasping for eternity onto projects of control and conquest. The Unique Self experiences authentically what the ego longs for mistakenly—namely the recognition that it is divine and therefore eternal.

This distinction is essential and therefore deserves a brief clarification. The separate self emerges at a certain stage of human history and at a certain stage in the development of the individual human being. As the sense of separate self solidifies, so too does the terror of death. The person feels correctly that death is wrong, that they should not have to die. They feel that they are eternal and should live forever. They are right. The core intuition of immortality could not be more correct. But locked as they are in separate self ego awareness, they misapply that core intuition in two ways.

First, because they are utterly identified with the ego, they apply their intuition of immortality to the egoic separate self. They think that the ego will live forever. Second, because they are identified with the now-eternalized ego, and yet at the same time are gripped by the fear of death, which is oblivion to the ego, they seek all sorts of Viagra-like identity enhancers.

They make the finite goods of the world into infinite goods. Money, surplus goods, power, accumulated pleasures—all become identity enhancers for the ego. Their purpose is to give the ego a felt sense of its immortality. But since the ego is not immortal, all of these death-denying immortality projects are doomed to failure.

Even though the ego does make these two essential mistakes, the ego's intuitions are not wrong. When the mistakes are corrected at the level of Unique Self, the truth behind those intuitions can emerge. After you disidentify with your separate self, your Unique Self appears as a distinct and indivisible part of the eternal one. It is in your Unique Self that you realize your immortality. The Unique Self expresses correctly the mistakenly applied, but inwardly correct, intuition of the ego.

25) Pleasure: Delusion or Divine

Money, power, and pleasure—when experienced at the level of ego—appear separate from the divine field and trap you in the clutches of grasping and striving. When experienced from the level of enlightened consciousness—money, power, and pleasure are expressions of your Unique Self touching the divine. Pleasure from the place of Unique Self is experienced as a divine caress reminding you that the world is sane and good. Ego pleasures feel narcissistic and solidify the coiled contraction into small self. They never satisfy; you are constantly driven to get more and more, and someone else's pleasure makes you feel your own lack. *The same pleasure experienced from the consciousness of Unique Self expands your heart and consciousness into the love-intelligence, love-beauty, and love-pleasure of All-That-Is. You are satisfied by even the simplest pleasure, and you delight in the pleasure of others.*

Similarly, power and money grasped by the ego seek to support the false belief of the separate self that it will live forever. Power and money are used to accumulate goods you do not need and to acquire superficial control over others in order to assure yourself that you are valuable and worthy. Money and power experienced from the consciousness of Unique Self are gracefully and skillfully deployed with delight for the greater good of all beings.

Separate from the divine field, money, pleasure, and power appear as foolish and even grotesque identity enhancers for the ego. This becomes radically apparent whenever we encounter death. The ego is confused. It fails to discern between separateness and uniqueness, and so the goods of existence are hijacked to serve its own impossible goal of survival—separate from the larger field of love-beauty-pleasure-intelligence from which it was never separate and never can be separated.

Correct intuitions that are hijacked and misapplied by the ego are contextualized and reclaimed at the level of Unique Self. These include eternity and the finite goods of the world, the goodness of pleasure, the divine aspect of power, and more. All of these are reclaimed without grasping at the level of Unique Self.

26) Ego Story or Unique Self Story Reloaded

Your egoic story can be taken away by the circumstances of life. Your Unique Self story can never be taken away from you. *Ego can be taken away from you. Unique Self can never be taken away from you.*

This realization was driven home to me years ago in a pivotal moment. It was a sweltering Thursday morning in Salt Lake City.

Three weeks earlier, my life had come to a careering crash. This was caused by a combination of circumstances that included my personal misjudgments or mistakes, and other people's misjudgments or mistakes. It was all driven by behind-the-scenes, masculine shadow, expressed in a strange combination of malice, ignorance, cowardice, and corrupt political maneuverings. False complaints had been made about me, directly encouraged by interested parties; and adversaries, playing on the hysteria and fear that envelop these kinds of events, had made sure—at least for a time—that there would be no forum set up to allow for any kind of due process, or even to hear and check both sides of the issue. Close colleagues and others in my circle, to whom I had given my heart and life energy consistently over many years, had turned away from me. Most were driven by fear, confusion, ignorance, weakness, and self-projection, with a very few of the hidden players motivated by the darker drives of power, jealousy, and legacy. As far as I knew at the time, I might never teach, write, or even see my friends again.

I was not at all sure that my body would survive the trauma. The broken-heartedness I felt was so fresh that I could barely function. The phrase "broken heart" is no mere metaphor. I felt the brokenness jutting out of my chest, feeling that at any moment I would explode into death from the raw pain of it all. Love and loyalty, the deep, abiding commitment to the best and most beautiful in another through whatever life throws at you, is what I stake my life on every day. The experience of love's betrayal was so intense for me that it literally took my breath away. My vocation as a teacher and fierce lover who tried to receive and honor the Unique Self of everyone who came his way seemed dead, trampled in the mud of false complaints and malice-driven rumors. I felt there was no way back to my path.

That morning, I was scheduled to meet with a law firm in downtown Salt Lake City that would help me determine my actions in response to the false complaints. I was staying with a friend some distance from downtown, and I had no car or any sense of direction in the city. I thought I would take a bus from the mountains to downtown.

Having cried most of the night, I pulled myself together and left the house around nine in the morning for my meeting at ten. But when I got to the bus station, it turned out that the next bus wouldn't come for two hours. I had no cell phone, not much cash, and no American credit card.

As I stood there, feeling totally lost, realizing that I wasn't going to make it to the meeting, I said to my heart, "My unique calling has been to receive people in the fullness of their beauty and to reflect back to them in radical love their goodness and greatness. How can I do that now?"

At that moment, a car slowed down by the bus stop, and the driver motioned for me to get in. I was confused. Why is this car stopping, and who is this woman motioning for me to get in? As I approached the car, a slightly plump fiftyish woman, with very lovely yet ordinary features and thick graying hair, leaned out and said to me, "I woke up this morning knowing that I had to leave for work early. I knew there was something I had to do, but I did not know what. Now I know. I need to take you wherever you need to go. Don't worry—I have plenty of time. Hop in."

I was more than amazed at this small act of kindness from a random stranger. I rejected the dark thought that perhaps she was a serial murderer, thanked her, and stepped into her car. We began driving toward downtown, quite a distance from where she had picked me up. I asked her name, which she reluctantly gave me, and then, my heart's curiosity naturally aroused, I started to ask her about herself. Slowly, bit by bit, she began to tell me her story. Before I knew it, we were both lost inside the lining of her story.

What a story it was! About a husband who had left her and having to raise three kids by herself. About her private but epic, tragic struggles with her boys. It was a story of love and betrayal, a story of love won and love lost, of a profound kind of pain and courage. It was a story that would have opened the most contracted heart. For the rest of the car ride, I forgot about my own pain, and lived and breathed inside her Unique Self story.

About forty-five minutes later, we arrived at the law offices. As she pulled over to the curb, still finishing her story, we were lost and found together on the inside. My heart was blown wide open by her goodness, her depth, and her heroic beauty in the face of so much suffering. My heart told me at this moment that there was only one real set of questions I needed to answer every day of my life: "Are you in love? Are you in love with the unspeakable beauty that lives in every person? Can you receive that beauty and give it back to every person you meet?!"

As she pulled to the curb, she was crying profusely. I had a tear rolling down my cheek, and I was not even sure why. She was a Mormon woman raised on the tradition of the tabernacle, high priest, and temple, and her next words came out of the context of her tradition. She looked at me and said softly, "Who are you? Are you the high priest in the temple? No one has ever listened to me like that and made me feel so beautiful."

Now, we were both crying for different reasons. As I thanked her and stepped out of her car, I realized that everything was going to be OK, even if it did not turn out well. I knew that while my ego could be crushed and my dignity debased, my Unique Self could never be taken from me. I could, wherever I was, hear and receive people's stories and remind them of their wonder and beauty. Nothing could ever stop that from happening. My Unique Self was inviolate. Everything else would find its way.

In the end, I did find my way back to my vocation—teaching, loving, and writing in the ways that have always delighted my soul. But on that day, I realized that the expression of Unique Self is not confined to what you do in public. It is not dependent on optimal life circumstances. Ego depends on these things, but Unique Self always finds a way to flourish. It is wonderful when life conditions meet you and support your most glorious manifestation. *You never know when the mystery of fragility will again intrude on your life. You do know that the apparent unfairness of the world can never take your Unique Self away from you.*

Ego Points to Unique Self

Ego is not the villain. All you ego-busters can sit down. *Your ego has wisdom to offer you. Ego holds truths that, in their clarified form, belong to Unique Self. The core truths of Unique Self are distorted by your ego's fear, contraction, and shadow.*

The following personal story is but one example of how the ego points toward Unique Self.

When I was 16, my teacher at seminary school, Pinky Bak, died. I was very close to him. Pinky was for me somewhat of a cross between a big brother and surrogate father. I came from a painful first thirteen years of life, and he felt who I was beyond the trauma. He said to me, "You have gifts to give. Your life is valuable. You are needed." He was the first one who invited me to believe in the possibility of possibility.

Pinky was thirty-two when he died. He fell down right next to me in the middle of a rollicking religious holiday party. As was his custom, he was dancing like a wild man—ecstatic, alive, on fire, and contagious. He half looked up for a moment and said, "Go on without me. I will get up in a second." He then died instantly of a brain aneurysm.

I was numbed with shock and my heart was broken. Later that week, the dean of the school asked me to give the eulogy on behalf of the student body, because everybody knew that I was very close to Pinky. The auditorium was packed. I was lost in grief because my teacher had died, and scared out of my mind because I had never talked in public before. But as I walked up to the podium, something happened. It was like a window from heaven had opened up. In my talk, the words flowed out effortlessly from a place beyond me.

They felt like wings, lifting and falling, carrying us all to a place where pain was not king, and broken hearts were healed. I spontaneously promised—not knowing where the words had come from—to pick up the baton that Pinky had dropped, to become a teacher of wisdom in the world. It was done.

The place was silent when I finished. Not silence of absence, when there are no words left to cover over the emptiness. Rather, it was Silence of Presence, when words are insufficient to hold the fullness of a moment. Although at the time I could not name the quality, this was my first genuine experience of Eros, of not only praying to or beseeching God, but of knowing that I was part of, not separate from, the larger divine field. In a moment of Eros, what I call in this book the Unique Self had shown its face. My Unique Self had shown its face. As it often does, it had made itself known in a peak moment.

And so began, at age sixteen, my calling as a teacher. As is often the case, however, my ego then partially hijacked my Unique Self revelation. I was, on the one hand, sincerely committed to teaching, sharing, and even evolving the wisdom of my lineage, but mixed with that sincere and sacred intention was an egoic need that used my speaking and teaching skill to cover up an aching emptiness. My childhood pain had not been healed or addressed. Instead, I had contained it, tucked it away in some supposedly safe place. This, I believed, was what a good person is supposed to do. I barely remembered where I had stored the container.

So public speaking and teaching, for which I had a gift, welled up from mixed places in my consciousness—from a pure instinct to express the good, but also from an isolated, vulnerable ego, passionately yearning for the wave of embrace and affirmation that came from the public's response to my teaching. At that point in my life, my need for a home and for the aliveness of public recognition unconsciously affected key decisions I made, but in very disguised and subtle ways. The good and sincere intention was so strong that I did not detect the ego's bad advice insinuating itself.

My false core sentence at the time was probably "I am not safe." When you have a false core, you develop a false self to soothe the pain of the false core.[68] The false self is precisely the

---

68 For an extended discussion of false sentence, false core, and false self see for example, S. Wolinsky (1999). Wolinsky focuses on the false core as that one conclusion you can make about yourself that organizes not only your entire psychology, but also how you imagine the world sees you and the false self, which compensates for this false conclusion. Volume 2 contains exercises, demonstrations, and protocols for dismantling the false core–false self complex

personality that you unconsciously deploy to hide, deny, or fix your false core. The paradox of the false self is that it usually reflects much that is true about you. The problem is that—at least in part—the false self is motivated by the ego's neediness and not by the authenticity of your Unique Self. The false self is false in the sense that it is not sufficiently motivated by the deeper truth of your own gorgeous and authentic being.

So if my false core sentence was "I am not safe," then my false self at that time probably sounded something like this: I am a rabbi, committed to outreach to unaffiliated Jews. I am filled with love, passionately committed, creative, and brilliant. I give my life to God. I serve my people and the tradition. Everyone is beautiful. I am committed to seeing only the beauty in people. If I just love people enough, I can do anything and take care of anything that comes my way. If I love people, they will feel loved by God. No one could possibly betray or distort my love.

Of course, none of this was fully articulated or even conscious. My false self was true, partially. But it was clouded by the ego's neediness.

I was asleep.

Part of what kept me asleep was—paradoxically—the depth of the teaching, the sincerity of my intention, and my sense of the innate goodness of others and myself. All of this was real, but it was happening at an early stage of egoic unfolding, when I was still—at least in part—identified with my false self. Since part of my energy was running in a false-self track; it ultimately could not sustain itself. The false self may well be telling the truth about your beliefs and intentions. But since it rests on top, and is motivated to hide, deny, or heal the false core sentence, "I am not safe," it never connects with the ground of your being and is therefore never stable or secure. I was headed for a series of dramatic train wrecks, with no idea that they were coming.

(unpacking the core teaching of seminal thinker Oscar Ichazo, founder of the Arica school).

Evolution Beyond Ego

In order to genuinely move beyond ego, beyond the false self—or even more precisely, beyond exclusive identification with ego—you need authentic and sustained contact with the transcendent, with the intention of facilitating your own evolution. You also need rigorous and unflinching self-inquiry, which includes some process of sustained shadow work. Prayer, chanting, contemplative study, and meditation are *part* of the path. In my early years, as for many young teachers, they were my entire path. But beware of parts pretending to be wholes. These paths may not be enough for you. They were not enough for me.

As I moved from my twenties to late thirties, my separate egoic self began to clarify through a mixture of chant, intense sacred study, and deep pain. By my early forties, the clarification process was becoming more intense and dramatic. But I still was not sufficiently clarified in the full realization of my enlightened Unique Self. Events then took place in my life of such pain and proportion that I almost died of heartbreak.

My own genuine mistakes and misjudgments provided a seemingly plausible cover to enable betrayal, public distortion, falsification, power plays, and behind-the-scenes malice. Whatever was not clarified in my person gave a hook to the projections of others, and my world came tumbling down. Held in the burning furnace of false complaints and public humiliation, by grace, I somehow remained alive. But for a full year, I could barely breathe. Not more than a half hour would go by without my heart welling up with tears. I was not able to utter the words of prayer. Only with great pain could I chant, and that very rarely. The visceral heaviness of my heart virtually stopped my life force several times a day. Enduring the pain of sudden rupture from all I held dear, the insanity of *National Enquirer*–like poisonous lies on the Internet,[69] for which there is little recourse, were more than the small egoic self of Marc Gafni could hold. The only analogy I can think of that holds the pain of that time is something like

---

69   See Solave, H. (2007). *The Future of Reputation*. Yale University Press.

the pain of losing the ones closest to you and then being falsely accused of their murder.

All of this came together as a gift of terrible grace.

I was forced to step out of my story. Out of my pseudo story. Out of my ego. Out of my small self.

All the spiritual work of the past twenty-five years came to my aid. But it was grace, known by many names, that shattered all vessels and cracked me open to a new level of light and love.

For the first time in my life, I found a place inside of me in which it was totally OK if I never taught again. I was able to locate myself outside of my gifts. I did not even know if I would be able to keep them. I was so cracked open that, for a long period of time, sitting in a rocking chair on the porch of some small house seemed like pure bliss. Pain, moments of loving, involvement in details of the world, spaciousness, taking refuge in the Buddha, and flashes of intense enlightened awareness all burst in at regular intervals—expanding and often dissolving my small self.

This went on for almost three years. And as time passed the vessel expanded.

I spent many hours in the first year after the tragedy reading Psalms, by myself or together with my friend Dalit. "Reading" is not quite the right word for what I did. It was more like intense wracked sobbing while reading the text as prayer.

I felt the psalmist and his God close to me, holding me, understanding it all, and lifting me up. And the gifts came back. At some point, I began teaching again, but from a more spacious place, a wider place. The meeting with nonexistence had worked me. The knot of the heart had been untied.

Yet it is not over. Knots can tangle up again very quickly. I untie the knots every day anew.

Something had shifted in a way that is virtually indescribable. It was, on the one hand, slight, modest, small, almost unnoticeable. And yet it was everything, all that is—grand and glorious beyond imagination.

I had experienced in a new way the depth of transformation that is possible when the ego opens up in sweet surrender to the luminous love-light of the One. Only then, after stepping beyond identification with ego—or more accurately, being thrown out of ego—was I able to take the next step. To truly live from Source as Unique Self, passionately committed to evolutionary manifestation, yet increasingly unattached to the results of my effort.

There was no choice. There is never really a choice.

So how do you live as Source? How do you allow your self to be lived by love as a force for healing and transformation? Not by leaving your story behind, but by entering the full depth of your story. Not your ego story—but your Unique Self story. It is on this essential distinction that your enlightenment and very life pivots.

What allows qualities that show up in ego to be reclaimed at the level of Unique Self is sustained contact with the transcendent, which shifts your perspective and opens the space beyond fear to do the genuine work of clarification and healing. This brings us back to our very first distinction between ego and Unique Self. In that distinction, I called contact with the transcendent True Self, the realization of your essential nature or the encounter with the second face of God.

Ego is pre-True Self or pre-Encounter.

Unique Self is post-True Self or post-Encounter.

Or at least, post some glimmering of True Self or Encounter, as both may show up in a flow experience or in other glimpses of authenticity. It is critical to also note at this juncture that, while True Self realization is the stated goal of most classic enlightenment practices such as meditation and chanting, contact with your True Nature may also be awakened through ethical practice, personal suffering or joy, transpersonal depth psychology, or other similar paths. After authentic contact with your True Nature—or at least a sustaining glimpse of it— garnered by any of these modalities or others, the gifts of ego can be harvested at the level of Unique Self.

Below are two examples of how ego points to Unique Self. Specifically, these examples include the gift of loyalty and committed activism, and the gift of passionate ecstatic entry into the invitation of the moment.

Glimmerings of these gifts appear at the level of ego, are clarified by contact with the transcendent through genuine psycho-spiritual work, and reappear with grace at the level of Unique Self. A simple deployment of the Enneagram typology model makes this point.

Let me say a few words about the Enneagram so that you can see how the gifts that show up in distorted form at the level of ego can reappear in clarified form at the level of Unique Self. Stated simply, the Enneagram divides people up into nine basic separate-self personality types. Of course, from the Unique Self perspective, every person is a type unto him or herself. Nonetheless, clear, broad classifications are helpful pointers in the right direction. Each Enneagram type is driven by a particular form of egoic contraction. In each type, the ego contracts in a very particular way, which produces a particular personality type, which has specific expressions of shadow and acting out.

While there may be some disagreement among the various schools of the Enneagram and their proponents, in all of them there is a clear evolutionary progression from the former fixation and ego-trap of each personality type to what becomes, through growth and integration, a positive expression of that personality type.

From the perspective of the New Enlightenment, you would say that this very same Enneagram type, when clarified and refined, reappears as what we are calling Unique Self. It is expressed in the Unique potentialities and gifts that this person might have to give, which are identified in their specific Enneagram type. The Unique Self enlightenment teaching which runs through these pages realizes that this evolutionary transformation takes place through contact with the transcendent, with glimmerings of True Self, which then allows the egoic properties to be clarified and reclaimed at the level of Unique Self. These are the great gifts of ego that point toward Unique Self. It is through this method that the shadow of your Enneagram type becomes the radiance of your Unique Self.

Example one: The basic primary egoic strategy for self-contraction of the Enneagram seven type, sometimes called "the epicure" or "the enthusiast," is to avoid pain and their own core wounds. The seven type can become terribly narcissistic and shallow in pursuit of fun, excitement, and distraction.

On the less wholesome end of the spectrum, this can lead to serial, never-ending, shallow romantic relationships, and oftentimes to addiction and premature death. On the healthy end of this same spectrum, the seven has overcome the fixation with fun, excitement, and surfaces, and has done depth work, confronted the primal wound, embraced their own shadow, and transmuted this repressed darkness into light and wisdom. The seven who has done this work then re-embraces enthusiasm, and sustained and repetitive passionate engagement with life, potentially becoming a model of radical, delighted, and even ecstatic existence in a way that is not dependent on external life circumstances.

Example two: The basic, primary egoic strategy for self-contraction of the Enneagram six type, sometimes called "the loyalist," "the trooper," or "the devil's advocate," is not avoidance, but fear. Their unhealthy strategy for dealing with this basic primal fear is often paranoia and vicious projection of the internal demons onto others, or in the reverse, their strategy is an extreme form of people pleasing that often involves a wholesale abandonment of principles and integrity. The type six is powerfully loyal, and in the service of that loyalty often abusive and damaging. The evolved version of these same qualities tends to produce courageous warriors for the sake of noble ideals who model service and almost unshakable strength, humility, and commitment to the cause of the good. The inner work of the six type is to confront the terrors within and without. In doing so, they are able to realize their own true essence beyond the fear and the terror that consciously or unconsciously plagued them in the past. In the most evolved case, they realize that their own True Self is none other than the source and wellspring of true faith and goodness. The thus realized type six accesses deep reservoirs of power and courage, becoming valiant, serene, and self-directed. The ultimate Unique Self expression of the type sixes who have faced their fears and transmuted them into a vibrant faith in life are the good knights and the fearless loving leaders who appear in the times of our greatest peril and need, rallying us by their example of courage and selfless service.

Conclusion

Our vision of Self matters. The story we tell about ourselves affects every dimension of our lives and loves. Our self narrative informs our ethics and shapes our Eros. The vision of Authentic Self or Evolutionary Self as an "awakened impersonal function" is all too easily hijacked to rationalize every manner of intimate violation by the ambitious builders of ego's empires, hidden behind the fig leaf of noble evolutionary motivation. While that, I am sure, is not the intention of the formulators or teachers of these dharmas of self, it is the organic, if unintended, consequence. This short book—rooted in the outrageous love of the infinite intimate subject—intends to fiercely, gracefully, and authentically amend the dharma by reclaiming the personal at the level of essence, emptiness, and enlightenment.

When I began teaching this dharma decades back, I was a lone voice. Even a few years ago, Unique Self was still being rejected as a Trojan horse for the ego. However, I am infinitely gratified to share that even the most abject opponents to Unique Self are now adopting it, by various names, into the core of their teachings. That is good for God. Not the God you do not believe in, who does not exist. But the God who is the Infinity of Intimacy. For Unique Self is not only your irreducibly Unique Perspective. It is also your irreducibly Unique Intimacy. For who are you other then God's Unique Intimacy?

Appendix A:

ADDITIONAL RELEVANT QUOTES FROM *EVOLUTIONARY ENLIGHTENMENT* (2011):

"[W]e seem to intuit a deeper sense of purpose that is infinitely bigger than our personal worlds can contain" (p. 3).

"When you discover dimensions of your own self and of life itself that are infinitely deeper and higher than your culturally conditioned, individuated self-sense, that 'personal' dimension of your experience is now seen as an important but small part of a very big picture" (p. 85).

"For far too many of us modern and postmodern men and women, embarking on a spiritual path has become just another chapter in the ongoing drama of our personal development" (p. 85).

"From a merely personal perspective it will always seem like we have all the time in the world... But from an impersonal, evolutionary perspective we *never* have more time" (p. 122).

"Those of us who have been culturally conditioned to see the world primarily through a personal lens..." (p. 123).

"Over time, as your practice and perspective mature, you begin to recognize that there are much greater, *impersonal* consequences to your victory or failure" (p. 122).

"But sooner or later we may fall back into a more familiar, unenlightened, personal sense of identity" (p. 59).

The passage goes on to make clear that the "relative self or ego" is the same as the "personal self": "If you have spent a lifetime identified primarily with your ego—with your personal story..."(p. 136). This is about being caught in your "personal fears and concerns" (p. 136) or the "narrow world of the personal self" (p. 137).

The ego "is also, however, our worst enemy, because today many of us have, as I have been describing, become so over-identified with our individual self-sense, our personal story" (p. 82).

For Authentic Self, the idea is to identify with the "impersonal creative energy" (p. 92), to move beyond the "the personal ego, the culturally conditioned self" (p. 126), and to realize that your essence is the "impersonal nature of the evolutionary impulse" (p. 93). This is contrasted with the living "from an individual or personal perspective" (p. 88) "when life is lived in a merely personal context" (p. 89).

"Could there really be anything personal about that pure, passionate aspiration to awaken, to become, to evolve?" (p. 42)

The idea is always to move beyond the relative "[a]s you awaken to the wild and impersonal nature of the evolutionary impulse, as your Authentic Self" (p. 93).

Appendix B:

STATIONS OF SELF FROM YOUR UNIQUE SELF (P. 54)

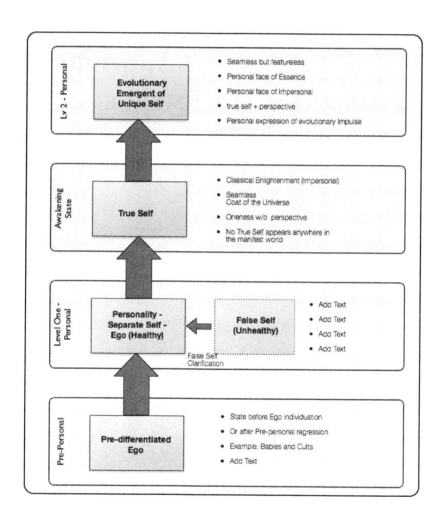

Appendix C:

TIMELINE—THE EMERGENCE OF UNIQUE SELF TEACHINGS

Unique Self is an original enlightenment teaching with antecedents in both Western and Eastern enlightenment traditions, and especially the Kabbalah lineage. It was developed principally by Dr. Marc Gafni between 1989 and 2012 in dialogue with Ken Wilber and numerous other dialogue partners who have contributed to its unfolding.

This timeline is also maintained at http://uniqueself.com/unique-self-timeline/.

SOUL PRINTS

- **1989** — Marc Gafni first taught "soul prints" at the age of 26 in a dharma talk at Delray Beach, Florida. The talk, delivered to five hundred senior citizens, communicated the Hebrew mystical intuition that our lives are infinitely and uniquely significant. He said for the first time, "Not only do you have a fingerprint, you have a soul print." In the soul prints book,

Gafni explicitly coins the term Unique Self and already, in a number of passages, talks about Soul Print not as a typology of ego, but as an expression of enlightened essence.

- **1990s** — Marc Gafni developed the intellectual framework of the "soul print" idea from research and teaching related to what he termed Nondual Humanism and the Unique Self in the thought of Mordechai Yosef Lainer of Izbica and in the Talmudic and Kabbalistic tradition from which he emerged.
- **2001** — Marc Gafni's book *Soul Prints: Your Path to Fulfillment* (Simon and Schuster) is published, becoming an international bestseller. Marc wrote about Unique Self in a number of contexts, including the point in soul prints: "The address of the divine commands us each to realize our Unique Self." In this context, he referred to the internal divine voice that lives in and as the interior face of consciousness. The book would later become the subject of a PBS special presentation. The book's scholars' page located a core source of the teaching in the teachings of Mordechai Lainer of Izbica.

Unique Self and Non-Dual Humanism

- **Early 2000s** — Marc Gafni expanded his Unique Self idea by writing the first draft of his doctoral dissertation at Oxford University under the co-supervision of Professor Moshe Idel and Dr. Norman Solomon. Gafni showed that for Lainer, an essential part of the process of what he termed *berur* might well be understood as a clarification of Uniqueness beyond the egoic separate self, that is to day, individuation beyond ego. It was in this work that Gafni clarified his own understanding of this process of *berur* as being about the realization of Self beyond ego or individuation beyond ego.
- **2005** — Marc Gafni formulated the core understanding of Soul Print/Unique Self as perspective, as emergent from Hebrew mystical sources on the ontology of perspectives. In this understanding emerging from Hebrew mysticism and from deep conversations with Ken Wilber, including

his radical emphasis on perspective, Soul Print/Unique Self was understood as the perspective attained at the post-egoic enlightenment level of consciousness. Gafni understood perspective to be a function of essence. Perspective and essence were in his understanding virtually synonymous.

- **2003 to 2006** — Ken Wilber and Marc Gafni entered into dialogue about the nature of enlightenment. When Marc sent his doctoral dissertation to Ken, Wilber evolved some of the implicit structures in his position, and in a series of conversations and emails, recognized the Unique Self teaching that Marc was articulating as a significant new enlightenment lineage that has much to offer Integral Spirituality. Ken in his early reading of *Soul Prints* understood it to be a spiritual expression of the separate self. This was an accurate reading of one strain of Unique Self teaching. However, in reading Gafni's academic work on Unique Self and Non Dual Humanism, evolved that teaching significantly. Wilber agreed with Gafni that Unique Self was a crucial evolution of the classical enlightenment teachings. Gafni also evolved some of the implicit structures of his position as a result of the dialogues, formulating the core understanding of Soul Print/Unique Self more clearly as a perspective. Ken's postmodern emphasis on perspective naturally dovetailed with the ontological kabbalistic emphasis of perspective, and together further deepened the Unique Self teaching. Dr. Gafni's teaching may be seen as emergent from Hebrew mystical sources on the ontology of perspectives and from his own realization. Gafni clarified that it is a perspective attained at the post-egoic enlightenment level of consciousness, and he identified perspective as an expression of essence.

INTEGRAL UNIQUE SELF

- **January 2006** — Ken Wilber convened a gathering of some fifty leading spiritual teachers for a series of translineage meetings at the Integral Spiritual Center (ISC). In a call with

Marc before the meeting, Ken suggested prioritizing Marc's term "Unique Self" over "soul prints" in his presentation so that the Unique Self teaching would not be confused with the separate-self/soul teaching of exoteric Western religion. Marc and Ken felt it important to move, in the Integral world, from the term "soul prints" and its third-person, metaphysical implications, to the term "Unique Self," which more readily expressed the first-personal realization in post-metaphysical terms. This was key in allowing Unique Self to be integrated into Integral Theory.

- **2006** — Ken Wilber invited Marc Gafni to give a featured address to the spiritual teachers attending the ISC gathering on the nature of Unique Self enlightenment. This was a key moment in Unique Self's emergence in the broader spiritual community. Many teachers wrote letters afterward saying that the Unique Self teaching significantly evolved their own understanding and experience of enlightened consciousness. Marc and Ken in their dialogues significantly sharpened the distinction between egoic individuality and post-egoic individuality. In the months after ISC, a number of teachers who were moved by the Unique Self realization began to incorporate it into their teaching, including Genpo Roshi, Sofia Diaz, John Forman, Diane Musho Hamilton, Sally Kempton, John Kesler, Vidyuddeva, and others.

- **2006** — Genpo Roshi and Diane Hamilton were also pivotal in the full transition in the Integral world from the term "Soul Prints" to the term "Unique Self." At some point after ISC, Diane Musho Hamilton and Genpo began to use the Unique Self voice when they were teaching the Big Mind Process.

- **2006** — Andrew Cohen and Marc Gafni shared a public teaching in Tel Aviv in 2006. At this point, Andrew rejected Uniqueness, saying, "There is no such thing as a Unique Spiritual Experience," and Marc's took issue with Andrew in an important exchange in their recorded debate. Through subsequent email correspondence and conversation, Cohen and Gafni gained greater clarity on the similarities and differences of their respective enlightenment teachings. Later, in 2010, Andrew and Marc would sit for a formal dialogue on the distinctions between Unique Self and Authentic Self, as part of the Future of Love series hosted by iEvolve and Integral Life.

- **2007** — Dennis Genpo Merzel, creator of the Big Mind process, which combined Western psychology and Zen, sees the publication of *Big Mind Big Heart* (Big Mind Publishing), a book which incorporated the Unique Self teaching into its framework. Genpo in a gracious written note explicitly thanked Marc for the Unique Self teaching, which he heard at ISC 2 and integrated into his Big Mind book and teaching. Marc thanked Genpo for the Big Mind voice dialogue process, which Marc incorporated into parts of his work.

- **2008** — Ken Wilber, Terry Patten, Adam Leonard, and Marco Morelli saw the publication of *Integral Life Practice* (Integral Books), which included a chapter entitled "Unique Self," directly derived from the Unique Self presentation at ISC, which Terry (who authored the Unique Self Chapter) attended.

- **2008** — Marc Gafni, Diane Hamilton, and Sofia Diaz established an organization, iEvolve: Global Practice Community, which intended to create a worldwide community of practitioners of an evolutionary spirituality with Unique Self as one of the key teachings.

- **2009** — In six weeks of August and the first half of Sept. 2009, Marc wrote the core 1,000 pages of material some of which formed the basis for almost all of *Your Unique Self* (Integral Publishing).

- **Dec. 2009/ Jan. 2010** — Unique Self further evolved the Integral space when Marc was privileged to initiate and lead an effort, together with Ken Wilber, Robb Smith, Diane Hamilton, and Sally Kempton, to reinvigorate the public practice space of the Integral Spiritual movement. The focal point of the effort was a series of annual Integral Spiritual Experience (ISE) programs/workshops. Because Unique Self had by that time begun to emerge as a new chapter in Integral

Theory, the event's inaugural gathering (ISE1) revolved around the teaching of Unique Self. In a series of dialogues with Lama Surya Das, Jean Houston, Alex Grey, and other luminaries, the teachings gained wider currency and acceptance. Marc wrote the core text for the Unique Self Teaching in the ISE material. The material was then edited and sharpened by Diane Hamilton. Marc together with Diane and Sally and the good persons at Integral Life, initiated ISE 1, 2, and 3.

- **Jan. 2010** — In the keynote address at ISE1, Marc suggested that the emerging movement must transcend and include the Integral world as it had been narrowly defined. It was in this keynote that Marc coined the term World Spirituality and put forth the vision that the order of the day was to evolve and articulate a "World Spirituality based on Integral principles." This keynote effectively began the latest recension of the World Spirituality movement. It unknowingly dovetailed with a theme of Ken Wilber's throughout SES, the search for the guiding parameters of a true World Philosophy.

UNIQUE SELF AND WORLD SPIRITUALITY

- **Dec. 2010/Jan. 2011** — The second annual gathering of the Integral Spiritual Experience (ISE2) put the spotlight on Love, using centrally the "Three Stations of Love" teaching that Marc developed in connection to Unique Self. This model emerged for Marc from the teachings of the Baal Shem Tov which was naturally aligned with a key developmental model which is core to developmental studies. Creativity, the topic of the third ISE, was initiated jointly by Marc and Diane Hamilton. In a key dialogue while preparing for ISE 3, Marc and Ken clarified the role of Unique Self and creativity.

- **2011** — The Integral Spiritual Center evolved into Integral Life Spiritual Center organized by Marc, Ken, Diane Hamilton, and Sally Kempton. Integral Life Spiritual Center evolved the Center for World Spirituality (CWS) initiated by Marc together with Ken Wilber. Ken Wilber played a role — by formal agreement with Integral Life — as "a supporter and leading voice" in the Wisdom Council of Center for World Spirituality and a key initiating energy in the formation of the CWS. CWS emerged out of the iEvolve: Global Practice Community originally founded in 2008 by Marc, Diane Hamilton, and Sofia Diaz. Integral Life and CWS split, and in a written agreement, signed by Marc and David Riordan at Ken Wilber's home, agreed to explore at a later date what the nature of their collaboration might or might not be.

- **2011** — Marc Gafni taught Unique Self to graduate students participating in programs related to Integral Studies at John F. Kennedy University. Hosted by the Chair of the Department, Sean Esbjorn Hargens, Marc delivered a keynote address at a JFK intensive which helped to solidify the importance of Unique Self teachings for the development as a critical new chapter in Integral Theory.

- **2011** — *The Journal of Integral Theory and Practice* (JITP), the official source for material related to Integral Theory and its application, devoted an entire issue to Unique Self. In this issue, Marc is the guest editor and writes two core articles on Unique Self, one emergent from Mordechai Lainer, and the other on the core Unique Self teaching, which are a cornerstone for World Spirituality teaching. Included in these articles is one by Zak Stein, which compares Gafni's Unique Self teaching with Andrew Cohen's Authentic Self teaching.

- **2011** — Marc gives a widely acclaimed TEDx talk on Unique Self at TEDx Las Vegas, which brings him into close collegial association with Eben Pagan and Wyatt Woodsmall, while introducing him also to Dave Logan. Eben and Wyatt join the board of Center for World Spirituality, and Dave joins the CWS Wisdom Council.

- **2011** — Kathleen Brownback introduced a new course at Phillips Exeter Academy in the spring of 2011, using Marc Gafni's Unique Self teaching as a framework for the high school students' education in religious studies. In November of the same year, her article "Teaching Marc Gafni's 'Unique

Self' Enlightenment in the Classroom: Reflections from a Phillips Exeter Class in Mysticism" was presented at the conference for the American Association of Contemplative Mind in Higher Education and was published as a CWS think-tank white paper. Marc gave a several hour intensive to the Religion Department of Exeter on Unique Self and the nature of Knowledge, which was later published as a department paper of Kathleen Brownback.

- **Jan. 2012** — Chris Dierkes publishes an article on the *Beam and Struts Ezine* website, "Unique Self, Authentic Self, and The Flavor of Embodied Enlightenment," fruitfully comparing Marc's Unique Self teaching with Andrew Cohen's Authentic Self teaching.

- **Feb. 2012** — At the second annual Board Retreat of CWS, over two dozen attendees chartered an expanded and renewed vision for World Spirituality based on Integral principles and sharpened the role of the organization as a think tank committed to evolving the source code of human existence in our time. Unique Self is a lodestone in that core vision.

- **May 2012** — A leading recovery/treatment center convenes a group of ten therapists to design a Unique Self treatment modality, to be implemented and formally measured and tested at the center.

- **May 2012** — Integral Publishing takes the lead in launching the Unique Self Integral teaching in the world.

- **May 2012** — A team is assembled to develop a Unique Self process which is to be launched online as part of a new Unique Self telecourse. There were two Unique Self courses offered prior to the new course and process, which were offered following Integral Spiritual Experience 1 in 2009-2010.

- **May 2012** — Marc has initial conversations with Ken Wilber, Zak Stein, Lori Galperin, Laura Wood, Richard Barrett and Don Beck and others about developing a Unique Self Index.

- **June 2012** — Integral Publishing published two academic volumes of nearly 1,000 pages called *Radical Kabbalah*.

Part I: Unique Self and Non Dual Humanism and *Part II: The Teachings of Mordechai Lainer of Izbica.*

- **Sept. 2012** — Integral Publishers brought out *Your Unique Self: The Radical Path to Personal Enlightenment,* the first book devoted to the Unique Self teaching.
- **Summer/Fall 2012** — Andrew adopted some key dimensions of the Unique Self teaching, which he had previously rejected, into his formulations on soul. Ken Wilber in a Guru-Pandit dialogue (Summer/Fall 2012) pointed to the possible source of these teachings in "Gafni's Unique Self teaching."
- **2013** — Awakening Your Unique Self tele-course and practice community is offered for the first time to wonderful reviews by students. Wake Up, Grow Up, Show Up, and Participate in the Evolution of Love telecourse follows the course with great success. Course participants step forward to take more active roles in the CWS community.
- **2013, Kurt Johnson in an essay identifying emergent new developments in Enlightenment theory cites Unique Self as key new development.**
- Evolultionary Christian Thinker Paul Smith writes a series of articles on Integral Life which are based in part on Unique Self thinking
- Between 2006 and 2013, Unique Self thinking directly and indirectly is adopted into the core structrures of teaching of over two dozen leading enlightenment teachers all over the world.
- **Sept. 2013** — Integral Theory Conference (ITC). Marc delivers an academic paper comparing the two models of self in evolutionary mysticism: Unique Self and Authentic Self
- **Fall/Winter 2013** — Marc publishes an ebook on Authentic/Unique Self, the two models of self in evolutionary mysticism. The book focuses on ten core differences between Marc and Andrew's positions and why the differences matter so much.
- **Andrew and Marc speak, coincidentally or synchronistically, two days before this book goes to press. Marc shared with Andrew his intent to publish this book, which was written in the summer of 2012.** Andrew evolves

his position tells Marc that after deep consideration he will incorporate Unique Self into his world view and teaching and Marc acknowledges gratefully the impact of Andrew's Authentic Self teaching on this own person and thinking. This served, from an authentic evolutionary mystical perspective as important example of genuine dharma dialogue which is at times sharp yet loving and respectful and always with the intent of clarifying truth in all four quadrants, at the highest altitude of consciousness possible.

NOTES

I. In the Authentic Self teaching, aligning with the evolutionary impulse is the essence of the teaching. Authentic Self is the awakening to what Barbara Marx Hubbard has called Conscious Evolution. Hubbard talks explicitly about awakening to the evolutionary impulse, which borrowing language from Swami Muktananda via his student Sally Kempton, lives in you, as you, and through you. In the twentieth century, this impulse was powerfully expressed in the writings of Abraham Kook, Sri Aurobindo, and Teilhard de Chardin, three modern evolutionary mystics. In the Human Potential movement, writers like Gerard Heard and others opened the doors for later writers—including Barbara Marx Hubbard, Michael Murphy, and Ken Wilber, who have each in their own unique ways championed the vision of an evolving enlightenment. Michael has spoken to me at length of his serious if cordial conflict for forty years with Richard Alpert, a.k.a. Ram Das, over Michael championing an evolutionary view of enlightenment. All three—Ken, Michael, and Barbara—are in part significantly influenced by Aurobindo and De Chardin and their schools of thought, an influence which they acknowledge with grace and delight. Murphy and Wilber are more sophisticated philosophers of evolution reaching back before Aurobindo and De Chardin to the German Idealists—Schelling, Fichte, and their colleagues in the late eighteenth and early nineteenth centuries, with Wilber then harking back at least to Plotinus.

Particularly key in popularizing some of these ideas is Hubbard's articulation of De Chardin, Aurobindo, Gerard Heard, and the evolutionary school is the notion of evolution awakening to itself through the awakened human being who realizes the highest levels of consciousness, thereby engendering an activist stance. In her book *Conscious Evolution,* Hubbard speaks elegantly of the evolutionary impulse and conscious evolution. Andrew Cohen's writing seems to be a beautiful articulation and evolution of this viewpoint. Schooled and awakened in a classical enlightenment tradition by a classical teacher, Andrew at some key point embraced the evolutionary viewpoint with a passion, integrated it with his classical enlightenment teaching, bringing his own powerful Unique Self to its articulation and evolution. Michael Murphy described Andrew's early ardent opposition to the evolutionary view and his delight and surprise when he heard of Andrew's own evolution in this regard. To be clear, this is a credit to Andrew's thinking and willingness to constantly reexamine his own assumptions.

Naturally, all of this evolutionary conversation takes place for each of these writers and for me based on our own context of realization and reverential receiving of what preceded us. Andrew has shared with me that his intuiting of the evolutionary idea in relation to enlightenment was something that he came to in his own reflection, which he later linked to earlier sources in the tradition of evolutionary spirituality. My own awakening to evolution comes through Avraham Kook, and his lineage source, Isaac Luria as I describe in footnote 10 and 14 below. It was amplified as I describe, however, by contact with the Integral Evolutionary thinkers and their sources.

II.   While Integral theory was not explicitly influenced by the kabbalists, Kabbalah profoundly influenced the German idealists Schelling and his student Fichte in the articulation of their evolutionary philosophy. This footnote in its entirety is adduced from Elliot R. Wolfson, *Language, Eros, Being: Kabbalistic Hermeneutics and Poetic Imagination* (New York: Fordham University Press, 2005), 392–393. The reason I cite it in its entirety is to ground in scholarship my claim, which I have put forward in public teaching for many years, that evolutionary spirituality is not rooted in the Friedrich Schelling school of German idealism. It seems to me more accurate to root evolutionary spirituality in the core matrix of Zoharic and primarily Lurianic Kabbalah, which greatly influenced Schelling and his colleagues. This however is not merely a question of historical accuracy. It is a far more significant question of the core source energy animating evolutionary spirituality. The kabbalistic source code of evolutionary spirituality gives it a depth and dimension that is critical to acknowledge and draw from.

From: Wolfson, Elliot R., *Language, Eros, Being: Kabbalistic Hermeneutics and Poetic Imagination.* New York: Fordham University Press, 2005. Pp.392-3.

On the influence of kabbalistic sources on Schelling, see Scholem, *major Trends in Jewish Mysticism,* pp. 409 n. 19 and 412 n. 77; idem, *Kabbalah,* pp.134 and 200; Schulze, "Schelling und die Kabbala," pp.65-99, 143-170, 210-232; Idel, *Kabbalah: New Perspectives,* p. 264; A. Olson, *Hegel and the Spirit,* pp.42-44; Schulte, "Zimzum in the Works of Schelling," pp.21-40; E. Beach, *Potencies of God(s),* pp.1-2, 6-13, 25-45, 22-230; Drob, *Kabbbalistic Metaphors,* pp.83-85; Gibbons, *Spirituality and the Occult,* pp.12-13; Kosolowski, *Philsophien der Offenbarung,* pp.565-771. On the presumed affinity between Schelling and Luria, see the important comment in the "Urzelle" to *The Star of Redemption* in Franz Rosenzweig, *Philosophical and Theological Writings,* pp.56-56 (see reference to Haberman cited p.57 n.23). In describing the "God that is before all relation, whether to the world or to Himself," the "seed-point of the actuality of God," Rosenzweig mentions Schelling's "dark ground," "an interiorization of God, which *precedes* not merely His self-externalization, but rather even His self," an idea that he further associates with what "Lurianic Kabbalah teaches." For analysis of the text, see Idel, "Franz Rosenzweig and the Kabbalah," pp. 166-167. Regarding the influence of Lurianic Kabbalah through the channel of Schelling in Rosenzweig's discussion on the first part of "Facing the Erraced," pp.75-76. See also the brief comment in idem, "Divine Suffering and the Hermeneutics of Reading," p. 151 n. 87. For the influence of Kabbalah on German thought, see Gardt, *sprachreflexion in Barock*, pp.108-128. The impact of Kabbalah on romantic figures, especially connected to theories of language, is also discussed in Kilcher, *Sprachtheorie der Kabbala*, ppp.239-327, and idem, "Die Kabbala als Trope," pp.135-166. See also Kremer, "Kabbalistische Signaturen," pp.197-221; Schulte, "Kabbala in der deutschen Romantik," pp.1-19; Cahnman, "Friedrich Willhelm Schelling and the New Thinking," pp.167-205. Also relevant is the monograph by Magee, *Hegel and the Hemetic Tradition*. The author duly notes the influence of Kabbalah on nineteenth-century German philosophical thought, largely transmitted through intermediary channels. See also O'Regan, "Hegel and Anti-Judaism," pp.141-182, esp. pp.156-172, 178-182. In this connection, it is of interest to note as well the passing remark by Derrida, *Dissemination*, p. 344, that the doctrine of T*sim-tsum*—the contraction into a point on the original ether—is "linked to the mythology of 'Louria,' but it can be arise by way of 'Hegel,' 'Boehme,' etc." And consider the passing parenthetical comment in Stuckrad," "Relative, Contingent, Determined," p. 906: "Schelling is an example of the deep impregnation of philosophy with religious ideas, for he described universal history in cabbalistic terms and spoke of *zimzum* and restoration." The thesis that Schelling's thought is a form of theosophic Gnositicsm was put forth by Jaspers, *Schelling*, and see, more recently, Kosolowski, *Philosophie der Ofenbarung*. The particular impact of Böhme has been discussed in R. brown, *Later Philosophy of Schelling*. A still-interesting and informative discussion of the mystical elements in Schelling can be found in Tillich, *Mysticism and Guilt-Consciousness.* On the question of Schelling's general mystical leanings and their impact on Heidegger, see Hedley, "Schelling and Heidegger," pp. 141-155. On the relation of Heidegger and Gnositicism, see chap. 3, n. 6, and for Scholem's engagement with and reactions to Heidegger, see Magid, "Gershom Scholem's Ambivalence," pp. 245-269; and Wasserstrom, *Religion after Religion,* pp. 136 and 310 nn. 60-61.

III.   In this essay I will deploy primarily key passages from *Evolutionary Enlightenment* published in 2011. This work is clearly described on the *EnlightenNext* official website as the authoritative statement of the Authentic Self teachings. However, the respectful and often lively conversation between myself and Andrew Cohen has roots that go back to a recorded conversation in 2005 in Tel Aviv. The conversation, which took place before some five hundred people in Tel Aviv, turned out to be our initial conversation on the nature of uniqueness. Andrew made the impassioned and articulate claim, repeated again in his audio series *Awakening to Authentic Self,* that "there is no such thing as a Unique Spiritual Experience." From the Unique Self perspective the precise opposite is correct. There is no spiritual experience that is not unique. A fruitful conversation then ensued in various forms, ranging from emails, telephone conversations, to in-person meetings, which culminated in a recorded dialogue in 2010, later published in dialogue form in *JITP* 6:1. I also included several footnotes in *Your Unique Self* with Andrew's written response to my critique as conveyed by his editor and student. I felt like the conversation was concluded when I published *Your Unique Self.* Sometime shortly afterwards, I picked up a copy of *Evolutionary Enlightenment* which Andrew had graciously given to my close friend and co-parent Mariana Caplan. In reading it, I realized that the issues I had thought we had drawn somewhat closer on through the years were re-stated there, in ways that required loving and respectful dharmic engagement. The Unique Self model presented in *Your Unique Self* and the Authentic Self model presented in *Evolutionary Enlightenment,* simply needed to be directly contrasted so that a reader might easily sense the differences. Although there are some significant emergent moments of shared understanding between the models that are not reflected in these books, since both of these books are regularly referred to as the classic and to some extent definitive statements on these two core teaching of self, I will use these books as my primary reference point.

Following this dialogue, Andrew and I have had some ten to fifteen significant conversations over the last eight years, including six significant recorded dialogues: meeting in Israel at my retreat location; in Fox Hollow, Andrew's center; on the phone; in a private three-way dialogue with our friend and colleague Ken Wilber; in a public three-way dialogue with Ken on creativity; in a hotel lobby in San Francisco; and in some email exchanges in 2005 and more recently.

There have been still more debates in the Integral world over Unique and Authentic Self. There have been to my knowledge five public debates in various parts of the Integral Evolutionary world over Unique Self and Authentic Self. These include a formal dialogue between Andrew and myself—a shortened version of which is published in *JITP* 6:1. There were two written comparisons of Unique Self and Authentic Self, by Zak Stein in *JITP* 6:1 and by Chris Dierkes on the *Beams and Struts* website. There have also been two dialogues, one between Sonja Student, the head of *Integrales Forum* in Germany, and Tom Steinenger, the head of *EnlightenNext* in Germany. Sonja represented Unique Self, and Tom, Authentic Self. This dialogue has been transcribed and published. And, finally, there was a dialogue in the summer of 2011 between Dustin DiPerna, a young Integral scholar/teacher, and Michael Haebacker, an author and student of Andrew's. All of these sources or links to them are available at UniqueSelf.com under the tab "Unique Self/Authentic Self."

At one point in 2010, I said to Andrew that the ultimate proof of Unique Self, which is not an awakened impersonal function, but the personal face of essence and the unique perspective of enlightenment, was none other *than* Andrew Cohen. Andrew laughed and said, "Touché." In the same light vein, I shared with Andrew that in the introduction to a recent volume of his teaching (2010), the book is described as his "unique perspective," a clear allusion to Unique Self teaching that was very different than where our conversation started in 2005. We both laughed, yet his formal position remained the same. In a formal dialogue transcribed in *JITP* (2011), Andrew limits uniqueness to a factor of social, psychological, and cultural conditioning.

Since these early dialogues, however, I thought initially that Andrew's position had shifted closer to the Unique Self understanding, which would make an article such as this unnecessary. When I wrote a critique of Authentic Self in *Your Unique Self,* I sent it to him and invited his response, which is the way that friends and colleagues should engage in respectful dharmic dialogue. A student of Andrew's replied for him with the following:

It is true to say, however, that Andrew does not overly emphasize this dimension of his teaching. In my understanding, this is more of a pedagogical matter than a philosophical one. Andrew's primary concern as a teacher is with helping people to move beyond the postmodern tendency toward narcissism and exaggerated self-importance that has become such an evolutionary cul-de-sac for our culture. In this context, I think he may be concerned that overemphasizing uniqueness either as a path or a goal might reinforce the very tendency he is trying to help people to transcend. As he puts it, "We tend to be much more familiar with the world of the personal self than we are with the cosmic context and identity of the Authentic Self. In our culture, in which the rights, needs, and significance of the individual tend to be held most sacred, the personal dimension has become imbued with exaggerated importance. We have become conditioned to seek the deepest connection to life primarily through the personal sphere, and, therefore, it is a profound step forward when we gain the ability to see this dimension of our experience in a context that infinitely transcends it."

The student continues:

I think Andrew's experience and teaching is that the flowering of post-egoic autonomy and uniqueness is something that happens naturally by itself when the individual lets go of his or her need to cling to the idea of uniqueness, and therefore it is not something he feels he needs to spend too much time on."

Andrew's position that he was using a pedagogical strategy to attack the narcissistic self shows an evolution in his thinking, and I fully received that response. It is cited in the footnotes of *Your Unique Self*. However, when I read Andrew's book *Evolutionary Enlightenment*, which is his definitive statement, he seemed to have reverted to his initial position that he took in our dialogue in 2005. He uses the word "personal" dozens of times in the book, and virtually every usage is pejorative and identifies the personal with ego and separate self. He also identifies uniqueness with egoic separateness. He does not seem to recognize the three levels of the personal, which move from personal ego self to the impersonal, and then to the personal beyond the impersonal, which is a quality of essence. Unique Self is not just another subtle disguise of the ego. Unique Self is rather the personal face of True Self.

Andrew and his student have leveled the critique that Unique Self is easily hijacked by the ego. This is a fair and important point. It is for this reason that in *Your Unique Self* I devote an entire chapter to drawing twenty-five clear distinctions between the experience of ego self and the experience of Unique Self. However, it is also worth noting that the ego can hijack the evolutionary impulse that lies at the heart of the evolutionary teaching that I share with Andrew, in the same way that it can hijack Unique Self. Discernment is always essential. Andrew and his students have also suggested that uniqueness is a natural expression, which emerges authentically after evolution beyond ego. While this is certainly true for some people, for most, clarification of uniqueness—including unique perspective, unique gifts, and unique obligation—is a lifelong spiritual journey of alignment with the evolutionary impulse.

As I was preparing this essay in the summer of 2012, a somewhat surprising and, from my perspective, welcome turn occurred in the history of the conversation between the Unique Self and Authentic Self teachings. As detailed above, there was extensive and substantive, if intermittent, contact and conversation about the distinctions between these two models over a period of seven years. The core Unique Self teaching was published in various forms ranging from its early form in *Soul Prints* (2001) *Tikkun Magazine* (2003), from the Integral Spiritual Center meeting (2006), to ISE 1 media collection on Unique Self (2009-10). The core teaching also appeared in *JITP* 6:1 in early 2011, containing my core essay on Unique Self along with Zachary Stein's essay comparing Unique Self and Authentic Self, as well as a dialogue between Andrew and myself on Unique Self and Authentic Self. Chris Dierkes's essay comparing Unique and Authentic Self appeared in *Beams and Struts* in January 2012. Oother Authentic Self-Unique Self dialogues mentioned above, took place in various different Integral contexts. Then, there was the Unique Self book, *Your Unique Self: The Radical Path to Personal Enlightenment* (Integral Books) published in late spring/early summer 2012. Three core expression of the Authentic Self teaching were published which included the Authentic Self Audio Series (2009, *EnlightenNext*), Being and Becoming (2010, *EnlightenNext*), and Evolutionary Enlightenment (2011, Select Books). After all of the above, in late summer 2012, two dialogues took place between Andrew Cohen and Ken Wilber. The second dialogue took place in fall 2012 under the title, "Resurrection of the Soul" (*Integral Life*, Nov. 2012), and the first took place in late August 2012, both after all of the dialogues and publications cited above and after the publication of *Your Unique Self*. In the dialogue on the Soul, Andrew took a very different perspective of the categories of the personal and unique. He again grouped them together, but identified them this time not merely with the separate ego self, but with the soul.

This articulation is precisely similar to the earliest version of Unique Self as expressed in my 2001 book *Soul Prints.* In the *Soul Prints* book, I deploy both the term Soul Prints and the term Unique Self somewhat interchangeably. I refer to Unique Self both as the individuated quality of emptiness or essence as in the later

Unique Self work and also talk about the unique character of the soul as a separate, unique (subtle body) entity. It is this latter usage of Soul which is the dominant model in that early version of the work that Andrew (independently) deploys in this dialogue with Wilber, locating uniqueness in this soul quality. This is a welcome evolution and marked shift in the teachings.

The more dramatic evolution of the Authentic Self teaching, however, takes place in an August 4th, 2012 dialogue between Ken Wilber and Andrew Cohen. One of my students who was somewhat surprised by the dialogue sent me a transcript of the dialogue, which I perused briefly in fall 2012, only reading carefully in May 2013 as I was preparing this article. There, Andrew articulates the core of the Unique Self teaching. Particularly, he talks about a level of uniqueness, which appears—as the core of Unique Self teaching asserts—after a realization of True Self. This is not the uniqueness of the soul, nor it is the uniqueness at the level of separate self or ego self. This is precisely the personal beyond the impersonal, Uniqueness beyond ego and soul, but as the irreducible uniqueness and individuation of essence that is the core of the Unique Self teaching. Ken Wilber's first response to Andrew's presentation seems accurate to me. Ken: "Well, in many cases, Andrew, this is somewhat similar to Gafni's and to some degree my notion of the Unique Self." Ken goes on to describe Unique Self, and they never come back to this point in the dialogue. Andrew later in the dialogue makes two distinctions, which are both core to Unique Self teaching. First, he points out that many people confuse Maslow's self-actualization with this level of consciousness— higher individuation beyond ego (which I have called Unique Self), when in fact Maslow's self-actualization takes places still at the level of separate self. This is completely correct from a Unique Self perspective, and this point is made many times in many different ways in the Unique Self writing. Second, Andrew points out that this level of uniqueness is not separate from, but is an expression of the process itself. This is—from a Unique Self perspective—also entirely correct. This is what I call Evolutionary Unique Self, which is "the personal face of the process, the individuated expression of the evolutionary imperative that lives in you, as you, and through you." (The fourth chapter of Your Unique Self, "Eight Stations on the Road to Unique Self" deals with this distinction extensively, as do chapters eight and nine on evolutionary spirituality.) None of these distinctions that Andrew makes in these last two dialogues in 2012, in which he expresses the core Soul Prints teaching and one which expresses precisely the Unique Self teaching, appear anywhere in the three core expression of the Authentic Self teaching that I reference above. They seem to be entirely new, and again from my perspective, welcome. If they are genuinely incorporated in the new iterations of the Authentic Self teaching, then this dialogue ends in agreement. At this point they are not incorporated in the core book of Authentic Self teaching, Evolutionary Enlightenment nor are they incorporated in the many of the re-presentations of Authentic Self, or what is sometimes called Evolutionary Self teaching. In a conversation long after this book was written, just a day or two before sending this manuscript to the publisher, in a conversation with Andrew in 2013, he made a spontaneous offering in regard to Unique Self. He said, give or take a few words something like, "I appreciate the respectful and loving nature of your critique over the years which was always about the teaching and never personal. I have considered it, and your teaching on the Unique Self is right. I was missing that piece." I appreciated his grace in this regard. I noted to him in that conversation the gifts his championing of the Authentic Self position had given my teaching and me.

It is perhaps worth noting my sense of how this developed as it says something important about how schools of thought emerge and influence each other. As I have already pointed out, the core idea of the evolution of God and the evolutionary nature of spirit is core to my lineage teacher Abraham Kook. As Prof. Josef Ben Shlomo already points out, Kook and Aurobindo (and in some respects Bergson) share much in common in terms of their understanding of the evolutionary imperative. Kook, who is a realized mystic of almost mythic proportions and significant scholar, kabbalist, and first chief rabbi of Palestine in the early twentieth century, is a central figure with enormous influence and not a fringe thinker in any way. Kook writes explicitly that evolutionary spirituality is the most accurate characterization of the kabbalistic understanding of the universe. All of reality, writes Kook—decades before cosmological evolution became a given—reality on every level—evolves. Evolution is, for Kook and Kabbalah, the core characteristic of spirit. The evolutionary nature of all of reality is the source for what Kook calls a radical affirmative "optimism." It is possibly noteworthy as well that the general lineage of evolutionary spirituality, which is sometimes sourced in Schelling (see, for example, T. Huston (2007)), almost definitely from a scholarly perspective, sourced in earlier Kabbalah. Eminent Kabbalah scholar Eliot Wolfson offers an overwhelmingly comprehensive bibliography, which documents the influence of Kabbalah on Schelling. (See footnote 11 above.) Secondary source readers like Huston Smith did not pick this up, and so the evolutionary dimension is entirely missing in his presentation of Judaism. Part of the reason for this is that the language, which is not explicitly evolutionary, marks the internal scholarly discourse on Kabbalah. It was Kook who adopted, in very explicit terms, evolutionary language. See footnote 14 for more information on how M. Kallus characterizes the Lurianic realization as being absolutely non-dual, one in which the human being awakens to his or her place as an incarnation of the divine process.

These ideas appeared in the writings of Aurobindo and Teilhard de Chardin in very similar ways, with apparently no connection to their early roots in Kabbalah and other evolutionary systems. Human potential movements icons like Ken Wilber, Michael Murphy, Barbara Marx Hubbard made this evolutionary understanding central to their thought, again independently of Kook. When Barbara Marx Hubbard writes of the Evolutionary impulse in her classic work, *Conscious Evolution*, she is clearly unaware of Kook and Kabbalah. Andrew Cohen has contributed a great deal to this conversation by both sharpening the formulations of evolutionary spirituality and especially in creating meditative enactments to access in first person an awakened experience of the impersonal function of the evolutionary impulse living as the

Authentic Self. When I came to this conversation some ten years ago, I was already deeply aware of Kook's evolutionary teaching. I was also heavily influenced by earlier kabbalistic works, like that of Meir Ibn Gabbai which talk in terms that "God needs your service," so this was central to my thinking well before I met the Integral world. However, Andrew's positive and clear articulation of the evolutionary teaching nonetheless added a new dimension and focus to my teaching and was not irrelevant in my turning more closely towards Kook's work on evolution. I am indebted to Andrew for this, as well as for the formulation of ecstatic urgency in describing the feeling of the evolutionary impulse. It is my hope that the conversations with Andrew and writings have had a positive impact and contributed to his recent formulations of the Unique-Self-like teachings. I am not clear if this expression of Unique-Self-like teachings was a genuine shift or a one-time exception. As mentioned above, a senior student sent me a transcript of the teaching, but in searching for it online in preparation for this paper, I was unable to locate it. The links that referred to it were not active. All and all, this is a positive story of natural and organic conscious or unconscious mutual influence, which is the delight of dharma dialogue and conversation.

IV. A. Combs and S. Krippner (1996) describe three basic notions usually associated with evolution: Darwinian evolution, historical evolution, and the growth of complexity and creativity in self-organizing systems. Hegel's system of the march of the process through time is an example of historical evolution, while Unique Self expresses different dimensions of all three. (See endnote 1 of Chapter 1 of *Your Unique Self* for more on Unique Self and growth through complexity, creativity, and self-organizing systems). Complex evolutionary theory was presaged by Bergson, Teilhard de Chardin, and Jung, according to Combs and Krippner.

The first of these, Darwinian evolution, Combs and Krippner explain as: "This idea, with its emphasis on the variation within each generation of, say, a bird or a plant, and the additional imperative that some survive, carrying their genetic heritage on to the next generation, while others do not, is clearly not what people mean when they talk of their own personal evolution, or even of the evolution of the human mind, or consciousness, through history." The second type, they describe as a movement of growth or ascendance toward higher and better forms: "Here we term this concept *historical evolution* because of its emphasis on experience and time. Sri Aurobindo's evolutionary spirituality, for example, is of this type. It is founded on traditional Indian ideas of a progress of the spirit through many incarnations, leading toward increasing identification with subtle levels of being."

Of the third general notion of evolution through complexity, Combs and Krippner say, "The recent rise of the sciences of complexity has led to an understanding of the amazing capacity of certain complex systems to evolve toward greater levels of complexity, and on the way to achieve increasing competence, flexibility, and creativity. Philosopher and systems theorist Ervin Laszlo has termed this third type of evolution *the grand evolutionary synthesis* because it brings so many kinds of complex growth processes together under a single conceptual roof. In a nutshell, the basic notion is that certain complex systems have the capacity to organize themselves into flexible and dynamic patterns of activity. They are said to be 'self-organizing,' and over time certain of them can grow in complexity through transformations of their own internal structures, leading to further increases in flexibility and complexity" (5-7).

V. In a Unique Self relationship, there is danger of excessive intimacy. This is not to reject the possible legitimacy and efficacy of intimacy in appropriate forms. It rejects, however, inappropriate intimacy. What the intimate relationship is between teacher and student must be negotiated between them and held by a circle of trusted credible persons beyond their own private agreement. It also and must be constantly open to revision and evolution.

The teacher honors the student as a Unique Self and loves the student as a Unique Self. This is core to the way I teach, live, and love. The core of the relationship involves a kind of "falling in love," for it is only personal love that can truly release the contraction of ego. For this reason, it is possible that on occasion such relationships will turn intimate. And they have. All of these relationships in my life have been with powerful adults. There were beautiful dual relationships. Some of them however went south and caused enormous damage to my life, family and teaching. However they were all, experienced at the time as attested to in voluminous correspondence, as mutual, powerful, and profound. Because of the cultural complexity around this issue I have come to believe that sexual relations even between adult powerful teacher and student are generally just not a good idea. For reasons that are in only part psychological but also cultural and pragmatic. Because of the complexity of this issue, I decided, as my default position not to have intimate contact with people in a formal student-teacher contract that was held between only me and only me. I essentially gave up my desire and predilection for privacy on the altar of leadership. I also allowed for carefully discerned exceptions, where intimacy has great value (and delight), and is not private. In these cases a third party or parties, generally a group of feminine elders, in trust and sacred container, hold the sacred intimacy. Because of this decision I also, in written covenant, ended the teacher-student relationship with anyone whom I had an intimate engagement with, in order to be faithful to my decision.

This brings me to a second issue of private relationships, which is a difficult and complex one. I have—my entire life, until 2011—always believed that private relationships were both possible and desirable. I drew an essential distinction between privacy and secrecy and critiqued the new age god of transparency, which ignored the postmodern insight that truth is contextual and that transparency can at best share facts and rarely share the nuance and depth of context. Indeed, there is a core contradiction between the postmodern call for transparency and the postmodern insistence that contexts create the genuine "truth" of reality. If context is critical, then sharing the facts—which is really all transparency can share—often distorts context. Since context is the essential truth of a situation, to be transparent is in effect to lie. Privacy becomes a requirement of truth. Postmodern liberalism in both spiritual and secular circles has been too caught up in its own self-righteousness to notice this core contradiction in its own ethics. Classic esoteric communities have always held a strong ethic of privacy. Indeed, the requirement for initiation into the mysteries has been the ability to hold privacy and not share the "secret." This requirement, which existed and still exists in many esoteric communities, is rooted in a profound psychological truth.

What causes a person to violate their own integrity and the sacred promise of confidentiality by inappropriately sharing something that they had committed to hold private? Often the commitment to privacy was made because something being held in privacy, if shared without a depth understanding of context, which is almost always how things are shared in public forums, could cause massive damage to the one of the parties or to others in their immediate or larger circle of intimacy and influence. Indeed, the English words "esoteric" as well as the word "mystery," most probably derive from the original Hebrew word *seter*. The word *Seter*, literally translated as secret or that which is held privately, has two meanings in Hebrew. The first, as we just said, is "secret." The second is "destroy." Why? Simply because the secret can so easily destroy.

Why does an otherwise decent human break a commitment to privacy and often wreak great damage on many people's lives? To compound the issue, the person who breaks their solemn commitment to privacy rarely takes responsibility for this potentially heinous violation. Rather, he or she uses the holding of privacy per se, in which the individual fully participated or even requested, as a kind of self-evident indication that what was held privately is necessarily morally flawed or abusive. That is often an absurdity, but because of the blind and superficial embrace of transparency by postmodern liberalism, no one challenges the moral violation that is often taking place when one side unilaterally breaks a sacred covenant of privacy.

The motivations to break the sacred covenant of privacy are several. A major motivation is the attention one receives for breaking the privacy and sharing the "secret." The one who violates privacy receives a major dose of direct attention energy, which is highly seductive. This is why one of the key tests of an initiate in the most spiritually advanced systems is, as we pointed out above, the ability to hold the privacy. Why? Because one who can hold privacy has a profound inner center of self. For that reason, the individual is not seduced by the hit of attention energy he or she could receive by violating the covenant of privacy and sharing the "secret." A second reason: If there is a three or four way circle of relationship and two of the people in that circle are holding a private relationship, either permanently or temporarily, for good and legitimate reasons, one of the two sometimes betrays the privacy. One of the major reasons for such a betrayal might be their fear that holding this privacy might adversely affect their relationship with one of the other people in the circle. When this is done unilaterally, without care and consideration for all concerned, it is an egregious betrayal and a heinous ethical violation of the first order. A freely entered into sacred covenant to hold privacy between two people is holy and must be honored, or jointly ended, but to end it unilaterally, in a way that damages one of the two original covenantal partners is simply heinous.

Of course, it is always true that a good value can be abused or distorted. Privacy has been wrongly deployed as a fig leaf for inappropriate secrecy, that is secrecy that protects all manner of abuse and ethical violation. Transparency in many cases is sacred and necessary. Genuine privacy has been distorted. Appropriate privacy is about holding secrets sacred. It is sadly all too easy to distort matters and portray secrets sacred as secrets sordid. When this happens, then the depth and sacred value of privacy are eroded to our great detriment both in terms of ethics and Eros.

There are many reasons to hold privacy. In my case, one of them was that for thirty years I was not able to fully integrate spirituality and sexuality in a way that felt fully whole or acceptable to the mainstream public. I have, since my early thirties, almost always had more than one intimate beloved. At the same time, with rare exception, I am essentially not promiscuous. Not on purely moral grounds. Rather, sex divorced from heart simply does not speak either to my Eros or ethics. For me sex has always been love in the body. Sex may be fierce and rough or gentle and tender, but it is always an expression of profound contact and love. I have always felt deeply connected and committed to the beloveds in my circle of intimacy. I have invested an enormous amount of time, money, life energy, value and commitment in my beloveds. Love for me has always created obligation and delight with the two never being separable.

Living a post-conventional relational life which is held privately and which contradicts the norms of the community you live and lead in is never simple. To be clear I never, not even once, taught one thing and did another. I never taught that conventional marriage was the only sacred context for sexing and always filled my teaching with implicit post-conventional possibility. I simply did not explicitly engage the complex issue of multiple models for relationship in my teaching because I did not think the communities I was in were ready for it. It was however not only the communities. I was not ready for it. I was myself profoundly Orthodox in many ways and at the same time post-conventional and progressive in many other ways. I did not yet know how to integrate both impulses. I knew that anything I said could easily be reduced, taken out of context and misunderstood.

Another reason that I held privacy and avoided these issues is that, in orthodoxy, even holding hands with one's beloved before marriage is understood by virtually every single authority to be a biblical prohibition. So that allows for precious little post-conventional erotic possibility. In human potential communities post-conventional possibility in most forms was politically incorrect in a pretty serious way.

I was myself conflicted on these issues, so therefore did not want to make these issues central to my teaching. I felt it would distract from a myriad of other teachings that felt more critical to share with mainstream audiences. Over the years, I shared deeply about my post conventional approach to relationships with a number of key leaders, who are still today high profile leaders in orthodox and more progressive circles and received some significant measure of support and encouragement. However my core policy in regard to these matters was always discretion and privacy.

Suffice it to say, in retrospect, this policy of privacy turned out to be, in retrospect, significant mistake—probably the most significant mistake of my life. Privacy was recast as secrecy. Secrets sacred were retold as secrets sordid. It is all to easy to mischaracterize simple privacy, held for a myriad of reasons, agreed on by both parties, as being "shrouded in secrecy" with all forms of negative and even sinister implications.

I also learned the hard way privacy was painful for people without genuine character strength, to hold, even when they professed at the time that is was totally fine with them. In the distorted dynamic of privacy, which is degraded by one of its partners into secrecy sordid, all sorts of wounds, hurts, and broken consciousness can fester and fume with highly damaging results. Moreover, holding privacy turned out to be much like handing your enemies a sword to kill you with. Privacy degraded, as a sordid secrecy allowed for a thousand distortions that could then be manipulated by people with agendas that suffice it to say, were not and are not, the noble ones that they profess.

I have written a blog post on this issue elsewhere.

In retrospect, although I stand by the need for privacy and the right to privacy, I have given up that right in my private life. For probably the first time in my life as of 2011, I simply gave up on any sense of exclusive relational privacy between any person and myself. I made a commitment, which I have not broken, never to hold privacy only between a person, particularly an intimate partner and myself.

I no longer have any private relationships. An appropriate level of transparency is simply better for people and prevents certain forms of wound and hurt. It also prevents people from using hurt in a private relationship as an excuse for attempting to inflict all sorts of damage. Sadly, this kind of self-protection is necessary as an ethical obligation not only to myself, but also to my family, students, employees, board, and general pubic. Hurt is a fig leaf behind which a thousand agendas are hidden. "I was hurt" becomes an excuse for inflicting the most atrocious of wounds. The ostensibly hurt can easily claim words like abuse as descriptions of their experience, particularly if the relationship was held privately. Post-conventional nuance, complexity, and audacity are then re-membered and re-narrated as conventional or even pre-conventional abuse. All too often, the one who falsely claims to have been abused becomes the worst form of abuser. Because of all of that and because of a certain blind spot that I sometimes have in discerning danger, I have refrained from all private relationships. All of my relationships today are in some sort of larger container of witnessing and holding.

REFERENCES

S.l. means no place of publication
s.n. means no publisher

Abe, Masao, and Christopher Ives. *Divine Emptiness and Historical Fullness: A Buddhist-Jewish-Christian Conversation with Masao Abe*. Valley Forge, Pa: Trinity Press International, 1995.

Almaas, A. H. [A. Hameed Ali]. *The Pearl Beyond Price: Integration of Personality into Being: an Object Relations Approach*. Boston: Shambhala, 2001.

Ghose, Aurobindo. *The Future Evolution of Man: The Divine Life Upon Earth*. Pondicherry, India: Sri Aurobindo Ashram, 1990.

Ben Shlomo, Yosef. Sheleimut vehishalmut betorat haElohut shel haRav Kook. *Iyun*, 33, no. 1-2, (1984): 289-309.

Buber, Martin, and Martin Buber. *Good and Evil, Two Interpretations: I. Right and Wrong; II. Images of Good and Evil.* South Carolina: Nabu Press, 2011.

Caplan, Mariana. *The Guru Question: The Perils and Rewards of Choosing a Spiritual Teacher.* Boulder, CO: Sounds True, 2011.

Cohen, Andrew. *Awakening the Authentic Self [the Path and Practice of Evolutionary Enlightenment].* [S.l.]: EnlightenNext, 2008.

_____. *Being & Becoming: Exploring the Teachings of Evolutionary Enlightenment*, ed., Ellen Dally, [S.l.]: EnlightenNext Inc., 2010.

_____. *Evolutionary Enlightenment: A New Path to Spiritual Awakening.* New York: SelectBooks, Inc, 2011.

_____. "I Just Called To Say I Love You: Reflections On The Multiple Meanings Of Love." *The Blog.* Accessed 13 May 2013 https://www.huffingtonpost.com/andrew-z-cohen/i-just-called-to-say-i-lo_1_b_822367.html.

Cohen, Andrew and Mark Gafni. "Authentic Self and Unique Self." *Journal of Integral Theory and Practice* 6, no.1, (Mar. 2011): 151-161.

_____. Conversation with author. Feb. 2006. Tel Aviv.

_____. Conversation with author. May 2005. Foxhollow, [?].

_____. Conversation with author. "Future of Love. Week 4." 17 Dec. 2010. *Integral Life.* Accessed [2014]. http://ciw.enfusionize.com/thought-leader-dialogues/future-of-love-andrew-cohen/.

_____. Conversation with author. "Future of Love, Week 9." 17 Dec. 2010. *Integral Life.* Accessed [2014]. http://ciw.enfusionize.com/thought-leader-dialogues/future-of-love-andrew-cohen/

_____. and Ken Wilber. "Kosmic Creativity." 27 July 2011. *Kenwilber.com* *Blog.* http://www.kenwilber.com/blog/show/700

_____. and Ken Wilber. "Ken Wilber and Andrew Cohen Speak On the Nature of the Soul: Resurrection of the Soul:" *Integral Life* https://www.integrallife.com/news/ken-wilber-andrew-cohen-speak-nature-soul

Combs, Allan and Stanley Krippner. "Jung and the Evolution of Consciousness." *Psychological Perspectives,* 33, no. 1, (1996): 60-76. Published online 17 Jan 2008. http://www.tandfonline.com/doi/abs/10.1080/00332929608405729#.VA4ww2Na92o

Degal, *Mahaneh Ephraim.* (1896). *Leviticus 25.* Brooklyn: [s.n.], 1967.

Dierkes, Chris. "Unique Self, Authentic Self and the Flavor of Embodied Enlightenment." *Beams and Struts: For Hungry Brains and Thirsty Souls.* 17 Jan. 2012. Accessed 13 May 2013, http://beamsandstruts.com/essays/item/770-unique-self-authentic-self-and-the-flavor-of-embodied-enlightenment.

Di Perna, Dustin and Mike Wombacher. "Mike Wombacher and Dustin DiPerna on Evolutionary Spirituality and Unique Self." *Unique Self.* 28 June 2011. http://uniqueself.com/unique-self-theory/deeper-dive/unique-self-and-authentic-self/mike-wombacher-and-dustin-diperna-on-evolutionary-spirituality-and-unique-self/.

Eustace, Cecil John. "Collected Letters of St. Therese of Lisieux." Trans, by F. J. Sheed. *Renascence.* 2, no. 2, (1949): 166-168.

Fine, Lawrence. "The Contemplative Practice of Yichudim." *Jewish Spirituality II,* ed. Arthur Greene, 64-98. 1987. New York: Crossroads, 1987.

Gafni, Marc. "Awakening Your Unique Self." Telecourse. 2013. Accessed 24 Nov. 2013. http://uniqueself.com/unique-self-courses.

_____. "Essential World Spirituality Teaching." *Ievolve.org.* 2011. Accessed 24 Nov. 2013. http://www.ievolve.org/essential-world-spirituality-teaching.

_____. "Evolutionary Kabbalah." *Marcgafni.com.* 2006. Accessed 13 May 13, 2013. http://www.marcgafni.com/category/articles/integral-evolutionary-kabbalah.

_____. "Holy of Holies with Marc Gafni." Private telephone session with author, transcribers Adael Elizabeth and Helen Bullock, 20 May 2012. Transcript in the hands of the author, Calif.

_____. Integral Spiritual Center. *Kenwibler.com Blog.* 21 Aug 2006. http://www.kenwilber.com/blog/show/122

_____. Privacy, Post Modernism, Sex, And Students. Marcgafni.com. (2011). http://www.marcgafni.com/resp/aaa-core-privacy-post-modernism-sex-teachers-and-students-on-sex-ethics-and-injury/

_____. *Radical Kabbalah,* Vol. 1. *Unique Self and Non-Dual Humanism: The Great Enlightenment Teaching of Ethics and Eros from Mordechai Lainer of Izbica.* Tucson, AZ: Integral Publishers, 2012.

_____. *Radical Kabbalah,* Vol 2. *The Wisdom of Solomon as the Matrix of the Enlightenment Teaching Of Unique Self And Non-Dual Humanism.* Tucson, AZ: Integral Publishers, 2012.

_____. *Re-Reading Ritual: On The Evolution Of Tears, First Steps Towards Integrally Informed Religion—The Model Of*

Rosh Hashanah. Preface by Ken Wilber. Tucson, AZ: Integral Publishers, 2014.

_____. "Sex, Ethics, Power: An Introduction." *Marcgafni.com*, 2008. http://www.marcgafni.com/resp/aaa-core-privacy-post-modernism-sex-teachers-and-students-on-sex-ethics-and-injury/

_____. "Sexually Incorrect." *Marcgafni.com*, 2008. http://www.marcgafni.com/resp/aaa-core-privacy-post-modernism-sex-teachers-and-students-on-sex-ethics-and-injury/

_____. *Soul Prints: Your Path to Fulfillment.* New York: Pocket Books, 2001.

_____. "Soul prints: Live Your Story." *Tikkun Magazine*, [March-April 2003]. 16(2), 33-40. http://www.tikkun.org/article.php/mar2001_gafni

_____. [Mordekhaï Gafni] *Ṭeviʻot neshamah: ha-derekh el ha-mitos ha-ishi* (Soul Prints), trans. Ḥayah Rimon. Tel Aviv: Yediʻot Aḥaronot, 2006.

_____. "The Art of Metoposcopy: A Study in Isaac Luria's Charismatic Knowledge." *Association of Jewish Studies Review*, 11, (1986): 79-101.

_____. "Ten Commitments of a World Spirituality Based on Integral Principles." 2013. Accessed 24 Nov. 2013. http://www.ievolve.org/ten-commitments-of-world-spirituality-based-on-integral-principles-by-marc-gafni.

_____. "The Emergence of the Unique Self Teaching." *UniqueSelf.com.* 2012. Accessed 13 May 2013. http://uniqueself.com/unique-self-timeline.

_____. "The Evolutionary Emergent of Unique Self: A New Chapter in Integral Theory." *Journal of Integral Theory and Practice,* 6, no.1, (2011): 1-36.

_____. "Unique Self." *Integral Life.* Integral Spiritual Experience I Media Collection. 2009-10. https://www.integrallife.com/store/integral-spiritual-experience-year-1-media-collection.

_____. *Your Unique Self: The Radical Path to Personal Enlightenment.* Tucson, AZ: Integral Publishers, 2012.

_____. "Wake Up, Grow Up, Show Up, and Participate in the Evolution of Love." Telecourse. 2013. Accessed Nov.24, 2013. http://uniqueself.com/unique-self-courses.

Gafni, Marc and Student, Sonya. *The Democratization Of Enlightenment.* [S.l.]: Integral Wisdom Press, [2014].

Gafni, Marc and Sean Esbjörn-Hargens. "Toward an Integral Theory." Date if possible Accessed 24 Nov 2013.http://ciw.enfusionize.com/thought-leader-dialogues/unique-self-the-integral-self/

Gallop, Jane. *Feminist Accused of Sexual Harassment.* Public Planet Books. Durham, NC: Duke University Press, 1997.

Graves, Clare. "Human Nature Prepares For A Momentous Leap." *The Futurist.* (April 1974): 72-87.

Greene, Arthur. *Radical Judaism: Rethinking God and Tradition.* The Franz Rosenzweig Lecture Series. New Haven, Connecticut: Yale University Press. 2010.

Habermas, Jürgen, Michael Reder, Josef Schmidt, and Ciaran Cronin. *An Awareness Of What Is Missing: Faith And Reason In A Post-Secular Age.* Cambridge, UK: Polity. 2010.

Heard, Gerald, G. Lowes Dickinson, and Sylvia Beach. *The Ascent of Humanity An Essay on the Evolution of Civilization from Group Consciousness Through Individuality to Super-Consciousness.* London: J. Cape, 1929.

Heschel, Abraham Joshua. *God in Search of Man; A Philosophy of Judaism.* New York: Harper & Row, 1966.

Hooks, Bell. [Gloria Jean Watkins] "Passionate Pedagogy: Erotic Student/Faculty Relationships." *Z Magazine,* (March 1996): 45-51.

Hubbard, Barbara Marx. *Conscious Evolution Awakening the Power of Our Social Potential.* Novato, CA: New World Library, 1998.

Huston, Tom. "A brief history of evolutionary spirituality." *EnlightenNext Magazine.* (Jan-Mar 2007). http://tomhuston. net/files/i35-EvoSpirituality.pdf

Ibn Gabai, Meir. *Avodat hakodesh.* Jerusalem: [s.n.], 1963.

Idel, Moshe. *Kabbalah: New Perspectives.* New Haven: Yale University Press, 1988.

Jacobs, Louis. *Religion and the Individual: A Jewish Perspective.* Cambridge: Cambridge University Press, 1992.

Johnson, Steven. *Where Good Ideas Come from: The Natural History of Innovation.* New York: Riverhead Books. 2010.

Kallus, Menahem. (2002). *The theurgy of prayer in Lurianic Kabbalah.* Ph.D. diss, Hebrew University of Jeresulem.

Jun Po Roshi [Dennis Kelly]. "In Defense of Promiscuity." www.integrallife.com. 2011. Accessed 24 Nov 2013. http:// integrallife.com/node/94238.

_____. "In defense of Promiscuity." *Integral Life.* 22 Feb 2011. https://www.integrallife.com/integral-post/defense-promiscuity-part-ii

Kipnis, Laura. *The Female Thing: Dirt, Sex, Envy, Vulnerability.* New York: Pantheon Books, 2006.

Kook, Abraham Isaac. *Lights of Holiness.* Jerusalem: Merkaz HaRav Kook: 1968.

_____. "Two Types Of Perfection." Jerusalem: Merkaz HaRav Kook: 1968.

Lainer, Mordechai Yosef . *Mei Hashiloah.* eds. Elhanan Reuven Golhaber and Yehudah Yosef Spiegelman. 2 vols. [S.l.: s.n.], circa 1854.

Luria, Yitzchak. *Sefer hakavanot.* Venice: Rabbi Moshe Trinki, [n.d.].

McIntosh, Steve. *Evolution's Purpose: An Integral Interpretation of the Scientific Story of Our Origins.* New York: SelectBooks, 2012.

Nagel, Thomas. *Mind and Cosmos: Why the Materialist Neo-Darwinian Conception of Nature Is Almost Certainly False.* New York: Oxford University Press, 2012.

Patai, Daphne. *Heterophobia: Sexual Harassment and the Future of Feminism.* Lanham, Md: Rowman & Littlefield Publishers, 1998.

Rolston, Holmes. *Three Big Bangs: Matter-Energy, Life, Mind.* New York: Columbia University Press, 2010.

Scholem, Gershom. *The Messianic Idea in Judaism: And Other Essays on Jewish Spirituality.* New York: Schocken Books, 1971.

Smith, Huston. *Forgotten Truth: The Common Vision of the World's Religions*. San Francisco: HarperSanFrancisco, 1992.

Solove, Daniel J. *The Future of Reputation: Gossip, Rumor, and Privacy on the Internet*. New Haven, Conn.: London: Yale University press, 2007.

Sommers, Christina Hoff. *Who Stole Feminism?: How Women Have Betrayed Women*. New York: Simon & Schuster, 1994.

Stein, Z. On Spiritual Teachers And Teachings. *Journal of Integral Theory and Practice*, 6, no.1, (March 2011): 57-77.

Storr, Anthony. *Solitude: A Return to the Self*. New York: Free Press, 2005.

Student, Sonya and Tom Steinenge. "Dialogue on Unique Self and Authentic Self." *EnlightenNext Impulse*, 6. 2012. Accessed 13 May 2013. http://www.ievolve.org/our-unique-and-our-authentic-self-tom-steininger-and-sonja-student-in-dialogue-translated-by-kerstin-tuschik/

Swimme, Brian, and Thomas Mary Berry. *The Universe Story: From the Primordial Flaring Forth to the Ecozoic Era--a Celebration of the Unfolding of the Cosmos*. New York: HarperOne, 1994.

Taylor, Charles. *Sources of the Self: The Making of the Modern Identity*. Cambridge, MA: Cambridge University Press, 1989.

Teilhard de Chardin, Pierre. *The Phenomenon of Man*. Trans, Bernard Wall. New York: Harper, 1959.

Tuschik, Kerstion and Heather Fester. *Distinctions Between Ego and Unique Self: Elaboration on the Original Distinctions by Marc GafniiIn "Your Unique Self: The Radical Path To Personal Enlightenment With Practices."* [S.l.]: Integral Wisdom Press, [2014].

Wilber, Ken. *Integral Spirituality.* Boston: Shambhala, 2006.

_____. (1995). *Sex, Ecology, Spirituality: The Spirit of Evolution.* Boston: Shambhala.

_____. "The Pre/Trans Fallacy." *ReVision*, 3, no. 2, (1980): 51-73.

_____. (1981). *Up from Eden.* New York: Doubleday/Anchor.

Whitehead, Alfred North. *Process and Reality.* New York: Macmillan, 1957.

Williamson, Marianne. *A Return to Love: Reflections on the Principles of A Course in Miracles.* New York: HarperPerennial, 1996.

Wolfson, Elliot R. *Language, Eros, Being: Kabbalistic Hermeneutics and Poetic Imagination.* New York: Fordham University Press, 2005.

Wolinsky, Stephen. *The Way Of The Human: The Quantum Psychology Notebooks, Volume II.* Capitola, Calif.: Quantum Institute, 1999.

Young, Cathy. *Ceasefire!: Why Women and Men Must Join Forces to Achieve True Equality.* New York, NY: Free Press, 1999.

1 Plotkin
2. Nov Emergence
3. D'G a Fni
4. J. Plotkin

- Uniqueness is expressed at the level of Soul AND personality
- The triple purpose of Life ∴ this retreat
  is to be free, joyful, & purposeful
- Personality experiences itself as separate-from-all
  → Soul   "   "   "   connected-to-all
      → personal autobiography v.s sacred autobiography

- Default Purpose - even mothering can be a default
      purpose, loving mothering is one thing
      being addicted to it is another

- 30 Disappear into the One & Appear as a unique exp
- Well... descending ego (not to Emptiness, but to Soul)
  is a legit path !... true self realization isn't
  required, just a cracking open of ego.

CPSIA information can be obtained at www.ICGtesting.com
Printed in the USA
BVOW09s2227261014
372422BV00022B/477/P

9 780989 682787